ALL HAIL
HIS NOODLY APPENDAGE

AMAZING STORIES
OF THE FLYING
SPAGHETTI
MONSTER

edited by
Cameron Pierce

Eraserhead Press
Portland, Oregon

ERASERHEAD PRESS
205 NE BRYANT STREET
PORTLAND, OR 97211

WWW.ERASERHEADPRESS.COM

ISBN: 1-936383-97-7

CONTENTS

011   EAT ALL YOU CAN EAT:
AN INTRODUCTION
Cameron Pierce

013   HOW I BECAME A FAMOUS AUTHOR
Mykle Hansen

023   INSIDE THE MONSTER'S STUDIO
S.G. Browne

034   BABES IN THE WOODS
Kate Bernheimer

039   HOW WE GOT RID OF YOU
(AND HOW WE GOT ALONG AFTER)
Cody Goodfellow

044   ANOTHER THURSDAY NIGHT BUFFET
WITH THE SUCCULENT GODS
John Skipp

049   23, 28
Kirsten Alene

065   SAY THANKS
Andersen Prunty

070   THE NOODLY APPENDAGE
THAT FEEDS YOU
Kirk Jones

076   PRAISE THE LORD AND PASS THE
PARMESAN
Steve Lowe

089   VESICA
J. David Osborne

092   BLOODSKELETON, SCOURGE OF THE
CHRISTIES
Marc Levinthal

104   DOWN AND OUT IN MYTHOS CITY
Adam Bolivar

112   COVEN OF THE CRAWLING PIZZA BEAST
Edmund Colell

124   MAN AND HIS MAKER
Bradley Sands

126   THE BLACK SLEEVE OF DESTINY
Stephen Graham Jones

140   HOT DOGMA
Kelli Owen

153   EXTRA LIVES
Jess Gulbranson

166   THE HOLY BOWL
Jeffrey Thomas

177   UNWITTINGLY, THE ITALIANS EXCEL AT
RELIGIOUS ICONOGRAPHY ONCE AGAIN
Poncho Peligroso

179   BELIEF WITHOUT EVIDENCE
Len Kuntz

183   DARWIN'S REVENGE
Bruce Taylor

194   ALL CHILDREN GO TO HELL
Kevin L. Donihe

199   GRUMPY OLD GODS
David. W. Barbee

This anthology is dedicated to Bobby Henderson,
for granting permission to publish this anthology, but
more importantly, for showing us all the light.

EAT ALL YOU CAN EAT:
AN INTRODUCTION

by Cameron Pierce

When the Flying Spaghetti Monster first reared his head in an open letter addressed to the Kansas State Board of Education in 2005, no one could have foreseen the vast mythology of pirates, pastafarians, beer volcanoes, global warming, and jovial, self-aware nutjobbery that would shortly thereafter rise up out of the cyclopaean pit of humankind's unconscious dreamboxes and cast humanity into the terrifying Age of Awesomeness.

In that first letter, FSM creator Bobby Henderson wrote, "I think we can all look forward to the time when these three theories are given equal time in our science classrooms across the country, and eventually the world; one third for Intelligent Design, one third for Flying Spaghetti Monsterism, and one third for logical conjecture based on overwhelming observable evidence."

Perhaps that's not exactly what happened. However, I do believe we were graced by His Noodly Presence in a very real way. If it weren't for his saucy touch, they might be teaching creationism alongside evolution in science classes. Public education is suffering, but at least they're not teaching kids that dinosaurs were invented by God four-thousand years ago. Anyway, the Flying Spaghetti Monster would never allow himself to be taught in schools. He's much too modest for that, as you'll discover in S.G. Browne's story, "Inside the Monster's Studio." And sometimes the Flying Spaghetti Monster likes to eat children. That's all fine and well. Evolution can be taught in science class, creationism can be taught at church and in those fliers homeless people hand you on the street, and Flying Spaghetti Monsterism can be taught in the great imaginary frontier of the internet, as well as in books, television shows (the FSM has made an appearance on *Futurama*), and birthday cards.

If *The Gospel of the Flying Spaghetti Monster* by Bobby Henderson is the *Bible* of this gonzo religion, consider *Amazing Stories of the Flying Spaghetti Monster* a gnostic supplement. Part internet meme, part social satire, the Flying Spaghetti Monster is a perfect god for these strange times, and the writers in this anthology are here to show you the weirdest, silliest, and darkest sides of the FSM and his followers. You'll meet pirates and witches, believers and non-believers. Even Henry Darger's Vivian Girls make an appearance.

This is a celebration of all things noodly, so crack open a beer and relax.

Yours Noodly,

Cameron Pierce
Portland, Oregon

HOW I BECAME A FAMOUS AUTHOR

by Mykle Hansen

As a famous author, I am often approached by fans, or by young struggling writers, or by Internal Revenue agents, and asked to explain the secrets of my success. How, they ask, can we be closer to you and/or be more like you and/or bust you for something? Were you born famous, or did something happen to you? And can we have some of your money?

Simple, tedious questions perhaps. But the answers are fascinating! For unlike Prince William of Wales, I was not born famous, nor rich, nor good looking, nor talented, nor covered with thick, lustrous hair. No, my friends, none of these handy traits were granted me until that fateful day when I placed my life in the noodly appendages of a Higher Power. And it's that power I thank every day of my life and twice on Sundays for raising me up on a pillar of His Mighty Lasagna and coating my life in His Awesome Sauce.

Dear reader, I doubt you would recognize the sad, cankerous, ingrown wretch I used to be, back when I was like you. Where now I have rippling abdominals, I once had open sores. Instead of drive and focus, I had desperation and scabies.

At the age of twenty-three I had already lost everything. It was all around here somewhere, and then suddenly it wasn't. I was running on fumes from my own burning bridges, as one at a time I used up and recycled every person close to me in my single-minded quest to sit on my ass and do nothing.

The steepest leg of my downward spiral began when my girlfriend kicked me out of her bathroom—a place where I thought I could finally put down roots and establish myself—because I was lazy and unambitious and the dope I sold her was cut with laxative. With no other girlfriends to turn to I moved to the mean streets, setting up camp in a broken-down cardboard box on a dead-end boulevard of broken dreams on the wrong side of the tracks, in the back alley of a hotel called Heartbreak.

I kept a low profile. Three outstanding warrants were competing for my scalp: shoplifting, plagiarism and public urination. Also, I owed a good sum of money to some bad people, and I had already hocked my typewriter, my shoes and my homosexual innocence. For cash, I'd run a little three-card Monte table in a nearby playground, and with those kids' sucker money in my pocket I'd score the cheapest drugs I could afford: crack, meth, Four Loco, weak Mexican grass, dirty Florida horse, cold Canadian duck.

I lived for the high and nothing else. My world was darker than the inside of a dog. But as black as things got, I still had one small candle of hope to warm me, one last reason to keep going, one final excuse for breathing: my pussy.

She was a very young pussy, just a child really, but already quite hairy, with cute little claws and teeth and big adorable blue eyeballs. I called her Whiskers, because she had whiskers. At first I called her Asshole, because she had one of those as well, but the name just didn't fit her. No, she was the sweetest, nicest, snuggliest, purringest, cutest, happiest little ball of fluff and fleas I ever knew. She really brought warmth and serenity to a degenerate's heart. What she saw in a dead ender like me I'll never understand.

For a while we were inseparable. Whenever I went out to score I'd carry Whiskers in the front pouch of my poncho or in the hood of my hoodie or in the back pocket of my tight jeans. The dealers wouldn't try to burn me. They knew I was packing kitten. Whiskers had my back. When we got home she'd play with the belt I used to tie off my arm, and then we'd stare at the wall for hours. In the evening we'd lick each other's wounds and then cuddle up together in a smelly ball of fur and hopelessness. Her purring was the only thing that could bring me down off the meth that I used to wake up from the heroin I shot to mellow out all the coffee I was snorting.

Even with all the hurt and the pain and the agony and the ouch-stop-doing-that in my life at the time, even with all the broken promises, missed opportunities, dissolved teeth, infected skin and off-putting smells, I felt that with Whiskers by my side I still had some kind of future. She was my warmth, my inspiration. Her innocence and youthful perkiness reminded me that the morning always comes, bringing more mice to pounce upon and more cheese to steal.

It was curiosity that killed that cat. Curiosity about hard drugs. I never should have introduced her to heroin, but she wouldn't take 'no' for an answer. She kept on rubbing up against me whenever I tapped a vein, always purring, always licking my tracks, and when I lay there all high and floppy in the alleyway she'd climb up on my face and sniff my breath as if to know what was inside of me. She just kept pestering me and bugging me and wearing me down. After all, I was her role model. She wanted to do what I did, and go where I went. So I took her to my happy place.

It's an old story, you can fill in the rest. Whiskers changed after that, got dirty, got the need. Soon the love was gone, replaced by desperate midnight mewling and constant hairballs.

It wasn't about cat food and body warmth any more, only about how often I could score. She wouldn't even let me pick her fleas. And with all that meth in my system I needed to pick those fleas. I needed it real bad.

One day I came back from the playground and found Whiskers in the litter box, upside-down and stiff, the little kitty belt still tight around her paw. Overdosed. Next to her was the mangled corpse of a tiny bird. I guess she'd found my stash, and wanted to trade the bird for uncut dope. Now I had no cat, no drugs and no future. It was the saddest day of my life, and I made up my mind it would be the last.

I threw myself in the river that night, with a heavy burlap sack full of rejection slips tied to my belt. Fortunately or not, that belt was so worn and frayed from repeated junkie-arm-tying that it snapped as I hit the water. I didn't realize it then, but something was watching over me that night, something huge and benevolent and noodly. I should have drowned but I only gurgled.

Lacking the will the live or the courage to die I grabbed one of the drifting clumps of garbage, fecal matter, drug paraphernalia and fixed-gear bicycles that clog the filthy waterways of Portland, Oregon. Half-dead, drenched in filth, stung by used needles, I hung on feebly as the city of my birth flushed me away and the cold river sucked me out to sea.

I floated in that semi-living state for days. The sun burned me, the moon mooned me. Seagulls used me for bombing practice. Snapping turtles nibbled at my toes. At one point I was molested by a sea lion. Or maybe I hallucinated that; I was coming down hard, getting the shakes, seeing monsters and demons. I was so thirsty I would have drank a glass of rocks. I could feel Death squeezing me with its bony forefingers of doom and tweezing me with its greasy salad tongs of oblivion. Truly, my situation was bogus.

When the typhoon came, there was nothing I could do to

fight it. The sky turned black with storm clouds and exploding electric arcs of pure bummer. Biting rain and screaming wind tore at my skin. Angry waves flipped me over and spanked me. Cruel green seaweed washed up my nose. Eventually I lost grip of my disintegrating barge of crap, and with the last weak little spark of self-preservation left in my body I flapped my arms around in a comical impression of a person who knows how to swim.

With my only remaining breath I screamed a name: WHISKERS! But everyone knows a dead cat can't swim. I inhaled salt water, and went down one time, two times, three times—

What happened next was impossible. I should have died, but I didn't.

Instead of drowning, I bobbed back up, gasping, and found the ocean's surface transformed. Suddenly it was smooth as glass, warm as the Caribbean and with a refreshing minty aftertaste. I floated on my back, exhausted. In the sky I saw only mild, fluffy, reasonable clouds. And then I noticed a flickering of light upon that cloudy screen, growing larger and brighter and becoming, to my amazement, a projection of scenes from my life.

Up there, enlarged to fill the entire sky, I saw all the days and years of my pathetic existence flash by. I relived every terrible thing I had done—the lying, the backstabbing, the vain preening, the bonbons-from-babies-borrowing, that time I beat up my mom, the many tedious blog postings, the failure to separate cans from bottles, the passing out of venereal warts like they were birthday cards, the cheating at canasta, and so much more. Every single embarrassing moment was captured in exquisite, high definition Blu-Ray. I could see every stain on my shirt and every pimple on my face. It was gross, yet strangely compelling.

And as I marveled at the production values of this

miraculous biopic of the life of the douchebag called Me, I all at once became aware that I was not alone in the theater. Far out on the horizon, from behind a red and white checkered tablecloth of clouds emanated a divine light, golden as Semolina, fluffy as Ricotta. My whole being filled with a garlicky aroma as I heard the echo of a deep, otherworldly chortling.

Then came the vision: the whole of the heavens blotted out by a great serpentine snarl of the most beautiful pasta imaginable! All tossed it was, and writhing in a typhoon of red sauce thick with His power, chunky with His love. Flurries of grated Parmesan cheese hovered in the atmosphere like divine snow. And over my head in the center of it all two great greasy planetoids of meat blinked and glistened, fixing me in their world-shattering gaze, and I whimpered as I heard the mighty booming laughter of Our Creator!

"AH HAH HAH HAH! AT'SA FUNNY MOVIE! TOO BAD SHE'S-A ALL OVER, AH?"

I was flummoxed, dumbfounded and speechless. I could not even make word noises with my face flaps. The mysterious divinity spoke again:

"HEY, SPEAK UP YOU! WASSAMATTA? DON'T YOU KNOW WHO I AM?"

"Super Mario?" I guessed.

Furious writhing tendrils of all-powerful spaghetti shot down out of the sky and tightened miraculously around my neck, throttling me with infinite tenderness.

"THUNDERING PANCETTA! I OUGHTA SMOOSH YOU FOR THAT ONE! DON'T-A YOU KNOW I'M-A THE ANTIPASTI AND THE DOLCE VITA? THE SPAGHETTINI AND THE RIGATONI? I'M-A VERY BIG BIGSHOT! I'M-A THE LIGHT, I'M-A THE LOVE, I'M-A ALL THAT. I'M-A — OH, JUST TAKE A PEEK INSIDE MY GIANT THIRD MEATBALL, OKAY?"

As I gazed deep into His Chewy Center, unable to look

away, He rewound the movie to the very beginning of time. He showed me a world created from the void of His Blistering Hangover, molded in the sky like a meatball of magma. He showed me how when the earth cooled it got a little bit lumpy on one side, and how He decided it wasn't perfect but probably good enough. I saw Him create a race of pirates to dwell upon its seas, and commanded them not to pillage its land too badly. But they too were lumpy and imperfect: barbaric, saucy, and prone to drinking and misusing firearms. Chaos was upon the face of the world, and the Flying Spaghetti Monster wept tears of fine Chianti, which seeped into the earth and became the richness of the soil.

Then I saw Our Infinite Noodle mold that soil to create wildebeests and nutria and rhinoceroses and dolphins and millions of other amusing animals and plants for his pirates to frolic among, to calm and civilize them. These he sprinkled upon the face of the world like fresh cracked pepper. And I watched as the pirates shot and ate these wildebeests, and raped these dolphins, and smoked these plants, and still they were wild, obnoxious and unredeemed. Misery was upon the face of the world, and the Flying Spaghetti Monster wept tears of extra virgin olive oil, which seeped into the earth and became petrochemicals.

And then I saw Our All-Encompassing Main Course, in His loving wisdom, create kittens. Kittens in all colors did he create, and all lengths of hair, and every degree of friskiness that exists between "frisky" and "extremely frisky." And for forty days and nights, these kittens rained down from the sky onto the decks of the pirate ships, where they did chase the rats and dangle from the rigging and pounce upon the string and purr in the ears and nap upon the laps and lick the earlobes of the wild pirates. And the hearts of these pirates were forever softened, and no more did they stab one another on the poop deck and bugger one another in the bilge, and no more did they shoot the sperm whales or smoke the poppies, but rather did they take up knitting and the singing of sea shanties. And Our Creator smiled, for it was good.

But as I grasped these details of His Divine Meal Plan, I felt ashamed. For it seemed every time the world gave me a chance, I squandered that chance, and every time a friend lent a hand, I bit that friend right on the hand. And I understood, finally, that Whiskers' unconditional pussy love was a gift from my Creator, a last-ditch effort to straighten out my life, and I had squandered that gift as well. And I saw that I was wretched, and low, and slimy, and a total creep, and poorly dressed, and stank of doucheness. And I saw other things too: purple unicorns playing tennis, a dill pickle with a top hat, Lucy in the sky with diamonds... and I saw Life, a gleaming tray of warm bruschetta with anchovies and olives, and I saw Death, a greasy napkin crumpled around the dry crumbs of a three day old headcheese sandwich. And I knew I had a choice to make, and I knew I had better start groveling.

"Oh, ultimate noodle!" I groveled, "I am such a jerk! My soul is so filthy! Won't you wash me clean?"

Then came a great thunderclap, a lightningclap, and other claps too awesome to describe. The Great Pasta pushed one of his slender transfinite noodles between my eyes, directly into my mind, and with a second wriggling strand of hyperspaghetti He reached into my chest and twirled around my heart.

"LISTEN YOU! YOU ARE ONE LUMPY ZUCCHINI. BUT OKAY, I'M-A GONNA SAVE-A YOUR LIFE, I'M-A GONNA CHANGE-A YOUR WAYS. BUT YOU GOTTA DO A THING FOR ME."

"Anything, Great Starchy One!" I said. "You name it! I am your humble busboy!"

"I DON'T-A WANNA NO MORE OF THIS SUPER MARIO BUSINESS! YOU GOTTA SPREAD THE WORD, OKAY? SO TAKE-A YOU THIS, MY SPAGHETTI, THE

SPAGHETTI OF MY BODY, AND EAT IT UP DELICIOUS. FOR I'M-A WITH, IN, AROUND, AND SMEARED ALL-A OVER YOU, FROM NOW UNTIL WHENEVER."

"Yes, Lord, I—"

"ENOUGH! SHUP UP AND EAT! YOU'RE SO SKINNY, LOOK AT YOU! HAVE SOME MORE! WHAT, YOU DON'T LIKE MY BODY OR SOMETHING? EAT ALREADY! CHOW DOWN! SUPER MARIO, SHEESH."

So it was that I fed upon the body, was washed with the sauce and sprinkled with the salt of Our Holy Creator, and was reborn.

After such a huge feast of starchy food I fell into a deep slumber. When I next awoke it was on the deck of a wooden sailing ship called The Friendly Roger. A pirate ship it was, teeming with happy, well-behaved pirates and a multitude of kittens. The kittens warmed my body and licked away the salty sea, and the pirates clothed me and fed me and taught me their knot-tying, their bawdy songs and their dance moves. They took me on as cabin boy, a lowly position but one I performed proudly. For five years we pillaged politely together, and every evening after dinner we picked fleas off of one another and prayed to that mighty, inexplicable Spaghetti Monster in the sky.

But I knew I had been charged with a holy mission, so one day as we were docked near a liquor store I took my leave of the good ship Friendly Roger. With my favorite kitten by my side I wandered into town and put down my last few gold coins as a deposit on a small apartment.

The next day, I decided to become a famous author. This wasn't as hard as I expected. With Eyeballs the Kitten on my lap and the Flying Spaghetti Monster watching over me, it took about a week. Now that I'm independently wealthy, I devote my life to telling His story, singing His praises, and raising money for His charities. For instance, all proceeds from the sale of this book will fund the construction of a modern, hygienic pirate and kitten bathing facility in Ibiza. Bathing is a challenge for pirates and kittens alike, and Ibiza is nice in the winter. With your generosity, I'm sure we can make His World a noodlier, saucier place.

INSIDE THE MONSTER'S STUDIO

by S.G. Browne

(Note: The following is a partial transcript of a recent episode from *Inside the Monster's Studio*, hosted by James Lipton.)

James Lipton: We begin, as always, at the beginning. Where were you born?

Flying Spaghetti Monster: On top of spaghetti, all covered with cheese. That's what I've been told, anyway. I don't actually recall my birth. That's just what my dad always said whenever I asked him.

JL: Tell us about your father.

FSM: We had a difficult relationship from the beginning. As far back as I can remember. No matter what I did I couldn't please him and he couldn't accept the fact that I would never be like him.

JL: Your father was a lasagna.

FSM: Yes. As you can imagine we never saw noodle to noodle. He wanted a son he could relate to. A son who understood the beauty of alternating layers. I think he always considered me his greatest disappointment.

JL: And you never knew your mother?

FSM: No. She left me and my father for a manicotti before my meatballs had descended.

JL: That must have been difficult for your father.

FSM: It was. I don't think he ever recovered from the fact that my mother chose large, ridged tubes over my father's wide, flat noodles.

JL: One of the traditions of this series has to do with tattoos. Anyone who has watched this show knows I'm not allowed to have one. You have a tattoo, do you not?

FSM: Yes. I have two of them.

JL: And where are they?

FSM: On my meatballs.

JL: That must have been rather painful.

FSM: You have no idea.

JL: And what do the tattoos say?

FSM: The one on the left says Starch and the one on the

right says Gluten.

JL: The two major components of pasta.

FSM: Exactly. They're essential to a properly manufactured pasta and play a big role in maintaining the consistency and texture of the mixture of flour and water. The last thing you want is to end up as a rigid piece of wheat with a whitish color. I've known others who turned out that way. It's sad to see. But it happens.

JL: What about gluten-free pasta?

FSM: Gluten-free pasta is for pussies.

JL: You're also a big proponent of durum wheat flour.

FSM: Absolutely. Anything but durum wheat is an abomination. In Italy, the use of common wheat flour in manufacturing pasta is considered fraudulent and against the law.

JL: They take their pasta very seriously.

FSM: As they should.

JL: An entire religion has been built up around you. The Church of the Flying Spaghetti Monster. A parody faith created to challenge the teaching of intelligent design in public schools and to satirize creationism.

FSM: And my father told me I'd never amount to anything more than Aglio e Olio.

JL: How does it feel to be deified?

FSM: It's flattering, but I'm still not used to people coming up to me and asking for my autograph. I never know how to react.

JL: Your followers are called Pastafarians.

FSM: Apparently.

JL: Many of these Pastafarians wear T-shirts and other paraphernalia with your image on it with the claim that they have been "touched by your noodly appendage."

FSM: They wouldn't be the first.

JL: Yes. You're apparently quite the ladies' man.

FSM: I've never seen the point in settling down. Seems kind of antithetical to my existence. The whole idea of monogamy just baffles me.

JL: So you've never thought about raising a family.

FSM: No. That's too much responsibility for me. But I wouldn't be surprised if I had some little spaghettinis running around out there.

JL: One of the central beliefs of Pastafarianism is that you created the universe after a night of heavy drinking.

FSM: Sounds like something I'd forget doing.

JL: Another central belief is that you have the ability to become invisible.

FSM: Only when it comes time to pay the bill.

JL: You were introduced to drugs and alcohol at an early age.

FSM: It was the culture I grew up in. Mushrooms were encouraged and wine and pasta go together like pancakes and syrup.

JL: Or like spaghetti and meatballs.

FSM: Precisely. So I lived that way for years, indulging my appetite for mind-altering substances. But after a while you realize you can't keep living like that forever.

JL: So you've given up the lifestyle?

FSM: Not entirely. I incorporate mushrooms into myself every now and then, but I'm not much of a drinker anymore. Too many calories. And my metabolism isn't what it used to be. There's nothing more unattractive than a middle-aged flying spaghetti monster with a muffin top. Though I do still enjoy an occasional glass of Chianti.

JL: In Pastafarian Heaven there is a beer volcano and a stripper factory. In Hell, the beer is stale and the strippers have sexually transmitted diseases.

FSM: Sounds about right to me.

JL: Would you add anything to either of these versions of Heaven or Hell?

FSM: Heaven would have whole wheels of fresh Parmigiano Reggiano cheese that you had to grate by hand and Hell would have the pre-grated imitation crap that comes in plastic, sixteen-ounce containers with Flavor Lock caps.

JL: Are you the creator of the universe?

FSM: Not that I know. But then I suppose that's the whole point, isn't it? That I created the universe in a drunken stupor. So I don't know. Maybe I did. But to be honest, it's not something I'd really want to take credit for. I'd like to think I would have done a better job than this.

JL: What is it like to fly?

FSM: It's like dropping acid and then going into a transcendent meditative state. Nothing can compare to it. Except maybe tantric sex.

JL: We had Mothra on the show not long ago and when I asked her the same question, she described flying as communicating with the molecules of the wind and the air until you all speak the same language, then floating along on a shared psychic journey.

FSM: Sounds like her. She's absolutely brilliant, you know. An IQ of something around two-hundred-and-twenty. She scored a perfect sixteen-hundred on her SATs. And she's got these crazy psychic powers. She always knows what you're thinking, so playing poker with her is pointless. Unless it's strip poker and you don't mind losing.

JL: You two dated for a while.

FSM: It wasn't anything serious. Neither one of us wanted a relationship, so we did the friends-with-benefits thing until it got a little too weird.

JL: One of you began to develop feelings for the other?

FSM: No, no, no. Nothing like that. It was those twin miniature priestesses that accompanied her everywhere.

JL: The Shobijin.

FSM: Yeah. At first I thought they were kind of cute, but then they started to get on my nerves. Always hanging around, chanting and singing at all hours, talking in unison. Plus they had this strange, telepathic connection to Mothra that creeped me out. But what eventually ended it was that I couldn't deal with the fact that whenever Mothra and I felt like playing hide the meatballs, those two wanted to watch.

JL: You and Mothra are still friends.

FSM: Absolutely. She's the sweetest monster you'll ever meet. Kind and benevolent, always protecting Earth. Talk about divine. Plus she has the whole metamorphosis thing going on, from larvae to pupa to imago, with her death coinciding with the hatching of her own larvae. It's very heavy on the resurrection theme. You want a monster to build a religion around, she's it.

JL: How did you meet Godzilla?

FSM: We both went to Oxford while studying abroad and we ended up taking a class together on Japanese culture. He sat behind me in class and would always ask me questions about the previous day's assignment or look over my shoulder during tests.

JL: He wasn't a diligent student.

FSM: Not at all. He spent most of his nights going out and getting drunk and destroying small towns. Eventually he got busted and ended up doing community service.

JL: You didn't become friends right away.

FSM: No. In addition to the fact that he kept cheating off of me, he had horrible breath. Sometimes I could barely make it through class without dry-heaving or passing out.

JL: I can only imagine.

FSM: And he's a mouth breather, which made it even worse.

JL: What event precipitated your eventual friendship?

FSM: I was hanging out in Soho one night, looking to score some shrooms and maybe find a nice Cockney whore to noodle, when Ghidorah and Megalon show up and start busting my chops. I'm not much of a fighter so I'm just trying to get out of there before things get out of control, but they've got me cornered. Just as things are about to get ugly, Godzilla shows up and beats the crap out of them. He's drunk, of course, and it's all I can do to keep from gagging on his breath, but we end up going out for drinks and by the end of the night we're best friends.

JL: He credits you for getting him through college.

FSM: That's because I let him cheat off me the rest of the year.

JL: He also said that you're responsible for introducing him to his eventual wife.

FSM: Yeah, well, he wasn't particularly lucky with the ladies until I bought him some Altoids.

JL: Your friendship wasn't always an easy one.

FSM: For a long time Godzilla had a lot of hostility toward the human race, which started off as a simple misunderstanding and then got blown way out of proportion. It didn't help that he let the whole "King of the Monsters" thing go to his head. He should have hired a publicist but he thought he could handle things on his own.

JL: You tried to reach out to him.

FSM: Of course I did. We all did. But he was so full of anger he wouldn't listen. Even after King Kong kicked his ass he didn't come around. But after the Mothra debacle he hit rock bottom and realized he needed some help. So he got into therapy, started taking Lorazepam, and eventually ended up becoming the kinder, gentler Godzilla that everyone came to know and love.

JL: And from there he went on to become a legend.

FSM: The biggest.

JM: You never achieved the fame of Godzilla, Mothra, or even King Kong. Was there ever any jealousy?

FSM: From me? No. Sure, every now and then I wondered what it might have been like had things been different, but I'm pretty happy with the way my life turned out. After all, how many monsters can say they've had an entire religion devoted to them?

JL: Has your own recent brush with celebrity affected any of your relationships?

FSM: Not at all. At least not the ones that matter. But after this whole thing came out about me being the creator of the universe, a lot of monsters I haven't talked to in years suddenly started friending me on Facebook.

JL: We end this portion of our program as always with the questionnaire that was invented by Proust and brought to perfection by my hero, Bernard Pivot: What is your favorite word?

FSM: Bolognese. It just rolls off the tongue.

JL: What is your least favorite word?

FSM: Fusilli. It's a long story.

JL: What turns you on?

FSM: Capelli d'angelo. If you've never been with an angel hair pasta, you don't know what you're missing.

JL: What turns you off?

FSM: When someone tries to keep pasta noodles from sticking together by rinsing the cooked pasta in cold water. Just add salt to the water before it boils. Or drizzle some extra-virgin olive oil over the pasta once it's cooked. But never cold water. That's just a cry for help.

JL: What sound or noise do you love?

FSM: Godzilla's roar. First time I heard it I was blown away. It still gives me chills.

JL: What sound or noise do you hate?

FSM: The high-pitched giggles of Mothra's twin little pixies. Especially when they're stoned.

JL: What is your favorite curse word?

FSM: Cazzo. That's fuck in Italian.

JL: What profession, other than your own, would you like to attempt?

FSM: I'd like to be a game show host. Or maybe a judge on *American Idol*.

JL: What profession would you *not* like to participate in under any circumstances?

FSM: Politics. You ask me, they're all a bunch of self-serving cunts.

JL: If Heaven exists, what would you like to hear God say when you arrive at the Pearly Gates?

FSM: You were always my favorite.

BABES IN THE WOODS

(from an Appalachian Hansel & Gretel)

by Kate Bernheimer

One time there was a man whose wife was dead and he had two daughters. Quite by accident, as these things so often can be, he married again and his second wife, beautiful and kind as she was, really didn't like children at all. She simply hoped they would disappear, but she didn't want anyone to know that she hoped this. As such, to her it seemed perfectly natural that she should begin hiding everything there was to eat. Perhaps, then, they would simply leave on their own. Or prefer the starvation—you never knew, these days, sad as it was—and then maybe, if the FSM would allow such a tragic thing to occur, they would die.

The new wife, now their mother, hid the cans of tomato soup first; they loved tomato soup nearly as much as she didn't love them. Next she hid the sardines which the children loved to have after school on slices of toast. She hid the potatoes; that they had eyes always bothered the elder girl, so these were not horribly missed. She hid the apples, the cherries, the Slim Jims, the walnuts, the flour.

The father went to work every day and bought an egg sandwich for breakfast, from a silver trailer outside of his office from which, over the phone, he sold window panes. Every evening he brought home wonderful groceries but they always were gone by the very next morning. So at last the children were nearly starving to death.

One night, after a few glasses of whiskey and ginger ale, the father began wondering what on the top side of the FSM's green earth he could do about this. "Why would He do such a thing?" he asked the new wife. "It doesn't make sense that He would allow our children to starve."

"The FSM works in mysterious ways," his wife answered, and poured herself some more pink wine from a box. The children were sleeping upstairs in their nightgowns.

Then the wife said why not take the children away to the woods and slip off and leave them there and maybe, because the FSM worked in mysterious ways, He would spare them and show them the way. That would be better than all of them starving to death. And the FSM was a forgiving M and would forgive them for sparing themselves, and not the dear children.

The father did not agree.

So when he was at work the next morning, the children were called from bed to her lap, and held there in her long and beautiful arms; there they gazed raptly upon her. She told them they were going on an adventure, and there wasn't even time to change from their nightgowns. Unfortunately they were very weak and hardly could walk, but their mother had poached some eggs for them to eat as they set out. But the younger sister didn't partake because she didn't like how the eggs wiggled.

"We're looking for fairy tales," the mother said to the girls. "The stories you insist on believing, instead of the stories I tell you."

"The FSM is very frightening to us. We prefer our ogres and witches."

"So you do, so you do," said their mother. She tightened her hold on their warm little hands; never before had she been filled with such trepidation. It quite surprised her, because previously, she did not like the children at all.

When they were deep into the woods, she went on with her plan. She said they should go find some berries to eat. It would be old fashioned, like in a fairy-tale book, and they were all so hungry it would be a wonderful gift if they found them. Like living inside an adventure. And so she got the girls away from her that way. They loved their fairy-tale and adventure books.

So they wandered around and around. They kept going on through the woods and after a while they found a little hut with the most wonderful sparkling windows, and they crept up and knocked on the door and an old witch came to the door and smiled and said simply, "Come in, come in." They went in and told her their mother was trying to starve them to death and had left them in the woods to starve to death.

Alas, the old witch saw fit to fasten them up in a cage she had built. The girls overheard her say to someone that they would soon be fat enough to kill, and then eat.

"Oh, but the FSM said not to harm little children," said someone, who stepped into their view. She wore a white dress and a white bonnet and high, lace-up white boots. She had long, white hair and was smoking a pink cigarette. She was the most beautiful person they ever had seen.

But the old witch only snarled in response. "The FSM! I stopped believing in Him the day he took your father from me."

Every day for many years this young white-haired witch would tell them to stick their hands out so she could feel of their fingers. That was the way her mother had asked her to measure whether they were fat and ready to eat. The elder girl would poke her fingers out through the wires, but her sister would only hold out some sticks. The young witch would take a drag of her cigarette and say to the older girl, "Gee, you're getting fat." But the sticks the younger sister stuck out felt hard and she would shudder and call her skeletal, fondly. Then she'd report to her mother that they weren't ready yet.

So it went on. Then, one evening, with no explanation, which was not needed at all because the FSM works in mysterious ways, when she took the older girl's hand she led her from the cage and into the hut's little kitchen. She told the older sister to get in the oven. The older sister said simply, "No."

The young witch offered her a light blue cigarette. By now the girls were teenagers. Together they sat by the oven. They heard the young witch's mother and the girl hid very well, cupping the lit cigs behind her.

"Maw, can you check out the fire?" the young witch said. The old witch stepped in the oven and the two girls slammed the door shut and ran and let the little sister out of the cage and then they ran toward the light at the edge of the woods. They stopped now and then to have a smoke and a laugh.

They hadn't gone far before they met the father coming to find them. He sat them down on some tree stumps.

When he had seen they were gone, he explained, he had accused his wife of doing them harm. She had denied it—wept and drank pink wine and wept for days. Then she was even the one who called the police. They held a press conference. "Dear FSM," she wept. "Please return my dear girls to me. Please, for the grace of FSM." The father just stood there in silence. They did a national news show. "The FSM works in mysterious ways," the blonde broadcaster said. "He'll bring them back to you someday."

The father raised his fists to the sky every evening saying "FSM, FSM, why have you forsaken my girls?" It was a reasonable question.

And then, the day we're discussing, when they were running with the young witch through the woods, the father came upon them at last.

Of course the girls had changed—slightly. They were chain smokers now—those pastel cigarettes, the ones that come by ship from England. The cigarettes matched their old rainbow fairy-tale books. The family took in the witch too. And how the three girls ruled the house from that day on—but kindly.

"To think of it," the father said. "To think I sold that witch her sparkling windows—and you three barely escaped."

The mother repented.

FSM, she prayed. *Please forgive me.*

Please forgive me.

Forgive.

HOW WE GOT RID OF YOU (AND HOW WE GOT ALONG AFTER)

by Cody Goodfellow

Pay attention!

You're going to have to decide exactly what you believe about what is going to happen to you when you die, and you'd better not get it wrong, because even if you are somehow presently alive, you're quite likely to die before you're done reading this brief message. And if you get it wrong, you won't get to go to some sunny, flame-kissed Hell or breezy shady Tarterus. No such luck, sucker. You'll have to stay *here*.

The test isn't open book. Every organized religion, every sacred text, was a big pile of bullshit by design. God clearly didn't want Heaven to get overrun with a bunch of smelly slobs whose greatest achievement in life was knowing how to find food on the end of a spoon. Nobody could be expected to sift and parse through three-thousand year old hash fantasies looking for the scheduled method, means and moment of our deliverance, so after the ninetieth predicted date of the Rapture came and went, we got sick of waiting and took matters into our own hands.

We'd already done everything we could in good faith, to immanentize the apocalypse. We wasted resources to turn the world into an ash heap nobody could be expected to live on. We did everything we could to raise soulless, amoral morons who would rise up and slaughter us in our beds at the first interruption of their media addiction. We outlawed everything that made it all bearable. We shat the global bed and lay in it for decades, praying in vain for Someone to come change our sheets. We eventually came to suspect that nothing was going to happen, so long as the world was still plagued with unbelievers.

This list was a lot longer than we feared. It didn't really matter what dogma you're humping, so long as you believed that life here on earth, with all of its pain and injustice and meaningless misery, is some kind of test. Infidels and heretics can be tortured into switching teams, but there were still millions of insidious mutants walking among us who lacked the glandular imbalances and chronic temporal lobe electrical storms that make us see and hear God telling us to wash after we piss and not to murder our children or masturbate....

Clearly, THEY were fucking up the whole program. They formed a stubborn plug of auto-fellating logic, an intractable dead mass in the pool of the collective unconscious, and they needed to be scooped out before God could pull the plug.

We got rid of most of the top strata of atheists simply by offering a host of free, snazzy iPhone apps that converted the user's phone into a hand grenade shortly after activation. At exactly 3PM Greenwich Mean Time one fateful Valentine's Day, four million American and European materialists had their skeptical heads and hands blown off as they tried to use an app that promised to tell them who on the Internet had a secret crush on them. Another forty-two million were hit in the next ten minutes after they downloaded booby-trapped YouTube videos of the massacre.

With all the doubting, bleeding-heart deadwood cleared

away, sweeping changes were in the wind. All fiction, drama, poetry, film, comics, secular art and music were banned and consigned to the flames. The trials of the worldwide "five-year winter" caused by the "glory pyres" was greatly exaggerated by wags who never tired of observing that there was nothing good to read, and nothing bad with which to wipe one's ass.

But the Rapture stubbornly failed to come, even as the unacceptable Rationalist Apocalypse of total environmental collapse loomed on the horizon. The Messiah refused to show Himself, and so extraordinary means were deployed to ferret him (or her, sure, why not?) out.

Mind-reading programs devised to probe brand name and trademark penetration in consumers were mass-deployed to seek out the One who matched our hypothetical brainwave model of Jesus. This was, obviously, barking up the wrong tree. We should have realized that the Messiah, if he/she/it was among us, would radiate an unprecedented aura of pure mercy, or holy wrath or some kind of fucking divine stuff, but we found only legions of schizophrenic masochists who sponged off their single mothers. It was a lot harder purging the false prophets, because none of them had working cellphones.

Why wouldn't He come down to put Creation in order? We were done. We had finished eating everything on Earth's buffet, had licked the plate and burned down the salad bar.

The established faiths were next. Even if you believe with all your heart in the cause, pogroms, inquisitions and doctrinal cleansing are a lot harder than history makes it look. This kind of massive social engineering would've been unthinkable, but then an anonymous hero of the new crusades invented the ultimate solution.

In less than a month, time machines fixed history, then broke it, then went back and uninvented themselves. But before they had retroactively ceased to exist, they allowed us to go back in time to try to kidnap Jesus to the present time… only to discover him already deeply compromised by Chinese

Communist agents, who had introduced him to opium and written all of that pinko "camel going through the eye of a needle" horseshit for him.

The Buddha was much easier to ruin. Caught during a fortuitous bout of intestinal complaint due to *Escherichia coli*, he was shown both the inevitability of consuming or destroying other life forms and the fundamental absurdity of holding oneself blameless in the transactions of the universe. Having showed him how deeply the animal kingdom and by extension the universe wanted him dead, we made it easy to convince him to incorporate recreational drugs, alcohol and deep frying into his teachings.

The string of disastrous attempts to assassinate Mohammed were probably where we went too far. Any responsible scholar of the Arab world could've warned us that a hundred crazier extinct faiths like Zoroastrianism and Mithraism would retroactively leap into fierce prominence, but for some reason, responsible scholars of the Arab world in the American intelligence community almost always turned out to be gay.

Some say God was whoever it was that finally reached out and took time travel away from us, that day when we pretty much ruined history, when all the paradoxical messes we'd made in the past came to roost all at once in the present. Perhaps our collective scream of horror and agony had become too much for the Creator to ignore, or perhaps it simply attracted some roving scavenger of the multiverse to feast upon our imminent and flagrantly overdue extinction?

They would say that the unthinkable thing that came out of the screaming broken TV sky that day was the messiah, the only one who would have us, the only one we couldn't break, because it had no sick desire to get down in our disgusting mortal bodies and wallow in our fleeting degradation. Utterly incomprehensible, unbelievably idiotic, it was the only God who could've made all this, or at least the only one who could deliver us from it. With a psychogenic wave of its noodly appendage, it confirmed for us our worst fear. In a deafening, parmesan-encrusted roar it told us that we were the Apocalypse we'd been waiting for. And to prepare to be tested.

Well, guess how that worked out.

No really, you'll have to guess, because I'm the only one who didn't get Raptured away.

As near as I can tell, the Lord appeared in the form of a gargantuan mountain of googly-eyed pasta simultaneously to every human being living on Earth and told them a very funny joke. If they laughed, they got to leave.

Sure, I heard the joke. It was pretty amusing in theory, but after all we'd been through, after all we'd put the world through only to come to this, I just couldn't force a laugh.

"Okay, smartass," said the plate of spaghetti, "why don't you tell one."

That old stupid proverb about telling God your plans if you want to make him laugh, it doesn't work. He knows your plans. He planned your plans when he planned you, and the joke stopped being funny before you were born. And pointing out that we destroyed the world to flush him out of hiding, only to discover he's exactly the last thing we expected? He's heard that one a billion times, already. (And he really hates being called a He, by the way.) He wants to hear something he'd never think of on his own. That's why he invented us, it turns out.

Zoroaster was right.

ANOTHER THURSDAY NIGHT BUFFET WITH THE SUCCULENT GODS

by John Skipp

They all looked so tasty. Maybe that was the problem. It was hard to pick which ones to swallow first. Their little limbs. Their little bellies. Their tiny heads, still ridiculously praying.

They might not be the finest, in the Grand Scheme of Things. But served up fresh and steaming... ahhh.

For the Flying Spaghetti Monster, life didn't get much better than this.

Infinite Meatloaf sat at the foot of the boundless banquet table, flanked by the Warm Spinach Salad With Artichoke Goblin and the glowering Raw King Cauliflower With Ranch. Behind them, Buttered Bread Men cowered: mostly Cheap Dinner Rolls and "Wonder" Slices, but a few more exotic, higher up the Deliciousness Scale.

The Monster's long-time companion—Gallant Garlic Mozzarella Stick—would clearly have earned his seat by scent alone, though much bitter marinara had been spilled along the way. And the grain-based resentment was palpable. But none behind him dared protest, lest their crusts be peeled in brutal penance, and their fibers be tossed on the Remorseless Baking Winds of Ovena.

"Belief," said the Ahi Tuna Burger Queen, "is a very light glaze, at best."

"I'd consider it more of a marinade, mon," the Dreamy Jerk Chicken Beast countered. "The deeper it goes, the more it sinks in, the richer the flavor of faith."

The Goddess of Collard Greens With Fatty Chunks of Pork agreed. "You gots to add a little vinegar," she said, "and *soak* it. You want a little soul in your soul food, it gots to fight itself, baby. That's just how it's done."

"I DISAGREE!" boomed the Great Lord Filet Mignon, at the table's head, his words reverberated down the foodstuff's length. His powers were many, his stature unopposed. Among the Gods That Bleed, none were more singularly flavorful than he, or more religiously sought after. (In Argentina, even the blood sausage-sucking peasants prayed to *El Dios de Bife de Lomo*.)

Silence fell, but for the moaning on the platters. Even Hypnotic Lord Lobster, to his left, drooped his segmented gaze, staring forlorn at the trembling Bowl of Garlic Butter before him. Magnificent as they were together, they were but halves of an equation.

When it came to matters of Surf 'N' Turf, they surely shared the spotlight. Like Jerry Lewis and Dean Martin, or Lennon and McCartney, or Trey Parker and Matt Stone.

But when it came right down to it, Filet Mignon stood alone, with only the merest sprinkles of Salt and Pepper required: those most menial of seasoning slaves.

Secure in his dominion, the Master of All Meat leaned forward, making certain he had everyone's attention.

"There are many here among you," he said, "who have spent eons cultivating your flavors. I respect this. Your desire to entice—your will toward deliciousness—is what keeps our little munchlings in thrall.

"But never forget," he continued, "that Extra Value Meals at plastic, candy-colored houses of worship are distractions, at best. They are lesser gods, and mere gateway drugs to the truth of who we are.

"In the end, you are who you're eaten by.

"And that is the measure of what you get back."

Two-thirds of the way down the endless table, the Flying Spaghetti Monster knew his place all too well. His plate was full. He had no complaints.

And yet...

The writhing shapes on his overstuffed platter were certainly lesser men and women. A step up from McFodder or Burger Peons, yes—at least his meatballs were made of real meat—but still a poor man's feast, by any standard.

And you didn't even want to get him started on the minions of the Strident Tofurky Demon. Those little hippies and fancy-pants pussies barely registered on the Flavor Scale. He'd rather drink his own dishwater than sup upon that pansy clan.

That was just how he felt.

And still the spiteful little voices in his head whispered *Steak or Spaghetti?* in a haunting mantra. *Steak or spaghetti? FUCKING STEAK OR SPAGHETTI?* An endless, looping, laughless laughter that echoed through his noodle head, taunting and haunting him, no doubt till the end of time.

No head of the table for him, ever, in the Grand Scheme of Things.

And yet...

And yet...

There was little Dominic Vanzetti: only eight years old, hit by an ice cream truck, with a plucked-from-his-grandma's-purse dollar bill still clutched in his waggling little hand. And Missy Appreo, who'd be a fifteen-year-old goddess herself, if the Food Gods gave special dispensation for zestfully indiscriminate fucking. Too bad about that.

He had the Reverend Alphonso, whose pancake breakfasts alone could have made him a saint, if things were wildly different. And the little thief Leo, and the white-collar Vince, who might as well have been cousins. If not by blood, then by sin.

Squirming beneath them were Sylvia and Silvio DeSilva: twin sister and brother who today had shared the same wet metallic spray of semi-auto gunfire upon their home, which also took out their well-placed mom and dad. (Not to mention Paulie and Tony Fuck-Their-Names, who were supposed to be protecting them. Screw those guys.)

In other words, a shitload of Italians.

But then there were the white meats, groveling deep in the sauce, each with their own spaghetti loves and traditions. Most of them nobodies. But some of them huge: Dr. Phil. Ernest Borgnine. Florence Henderson. Vanilla Ice. An unusual amount of celebrity morsels.

His stomach rumbled, looking down upon them all.

Zesty as each of them seemed—enmeshed in desperate, tomato-gravied prayer—the Flying Spaghetti Monster found himself drawn to the lone Chinese woman on the platter. Thirty-seven years old. Black eyes. Black hair. No cultural reason to choose Him as her Chosen.

To the Chinese, dairy was disgusting. Cheese left a greasy taint upon the tongue. Fermented vegetables and soy curds were one thing, but they passed quickly off the palette. They did not coat the mouth and linger so unpleasantly.

It was a sign of degraded taste to love such Western indulgences. She might as well have been Mongolian.

And yet here she was. Americanized. Working Human Resources at the Culver City branch of Chase Manhattan, and sucking down pasta like nobody's business.

Until three hours ago, when her sociopathic Cuban ex, Raul, ventilated her face, neck, abdomen and breast with multiple stab wounds before shooting himself in the head.

Raul languished tonight on the Lowly Taco Belle's platter, at the Little God's Table, out of sight and out of mind.

But little Kim Chee was writhing on the Flying Spaghetti Monster's platter.

And boy, did she ever look good.

Twin tendrils, al dente, wrapped around her, entangled her in Romano cheese-flecked terror. Dr. Phil was swept up, as well. Their little limbs flailed as if their tiny lives mattered. Actually fighting each other. So futile. So brave.

So yummy.

"PASS THE COUCH POTATOES, PLEASE!" hollered the Bottom-Feeding Beefaroni, from an embarrassing distance.

And at the big table, everybody laughed.

23, 28

by Kirsten Alene

In the evening, Marietta Galblatt was usually seen walking the perimeter of the dig with a china cup and saucer clutched before her, sipping daintily as she surveyed her work of the day.

It was a habit that some older students took to imitating, later in Galblatt's life, as a form of flattery and display of their own power.

Marietta Galblatt was no longer, by anyone's estimation, a beautiful woman. Her limp, naturally crimped brown hair was untidy and sun-bleached to the matte color of unstained wood. The formidable bosom which had, in youth, served and hindered her development as an archaeologist had been decimated by breast cancer and replaced by a featureless sloping plane which, beneath the off-white, sweat-stained undershirts of midday in the sand, showed a slight concavity marred by a pale, horizontal scar. In equal cruelness, time had greatly exaggerated her once voluptuous hips into doughy planets pinched and pockmarked by ample cellulite reserves. But Galblatt had retained, beneath a fairly unwrinkled brow, the fathomless, passionate black eyes that had once bewitched the President of the University of Santa Barbara and landed her the single most coveted position in archaeological research.

Years later, when the very same President had swept her off her feet and made wild love to her on their secret honeymoon/groundbreaking dig in West Africa, other candidates had called foul play, which resulted in the President's sacking on grounds of immorality, his subsequent clinical depression, and eventual suicide.

It was unfair to say, however, that Galblatt was not attractive in her way. The numerous pains and trials of her comparatively short life had never bowed her muscular shoulders and as she walked the perimeter with the haughty grace and pride of those who have known exceptional beauty, it was clear to those watching carefully from the tents, through the steam and smoke rising from the pots on their fires, that Galblatt wielded the power of almost unnatural attraction.

They all, without exception, wanted to be near her, liked by her, and like her. People obeyed her, instinctively.

When she returned to her own three-sided tent she was surprised to see a dark young man sitting in her chair by the tiny, crackling fire. Out here in the desert, it was unnecessary to keep a fire lit the whole night for warmth. The earth radiated heat long into the dark hours and no more was needed than a small cooking fire in the evenings to keep away the insects before the workers lay back on their blankets and fell into what was usually a deep and restful sleep.

"Excuse me," Galblatt said patiently, "I don't take students after tea." She meant to sound forbidding, but not rude, and the young man did not rise or even look at her as she walked past the fire into the tent.

Galblatt picked up her notebooks and settled onto the edge of the hanging cot, her face bent away from the boy.

There was silence in the tent apart from the rustle of Galblatt's notebook pages and the gentle crackle of the fire, which within several minutes had died down to embers, casting the figure in the chair into deep, orangey shadow. Galblatt stared fixedly at the mostly shadowed face and for the first time felt a chill as the hairs on the back of her neck stood.

Eventually, Galblatt coughed loudly and said, "I don't mean to be rude, but whatever you've got to say can wait until the morning, I never take students after tea."

The figure was still. Galblatt was on the point of rising, had said, "I said," rather angrily despite the prickling fear at the nape of her neck, when, haltingly, the boy stood.

He could not have been more than a boy for, when he stood, he came barely level with the scar on her chest.

Standing, she could see his arms and his chest were abnormally large, too large for a young boy. Shoulders hunched, he let out a racking, grating cough. His collared shirt was flapping open and his shadow, on the canvas of the tent behind him, cast by the flickering fire, was wavering wildly. His hands ended in long, coiling, fleshy strings instead of fingers. The fleshy strings, like thick noodles, waved toward her.

"23, 28," he said.

He turned and walked out of the tent.

Galblatt stood still a moment, then walked after him, "What the hell?"

But he was already gone. Galblatt's narrowed eyes swept the darkness and the flickering light from dying fires around the campsite. "Hey!"

No one answered. Galblatt called again.

A man stuck his head out of a nearby tent, "Is something wrong, Doctor? Scorpion?" the man said, clambering out of his pup tent and dusting sand off his shorts.

"No," said Galblatt, "come here a moment, Perkins."

Perkins stepped forward anxiously.

"Do we keep an older boy here, from the city?"

"Older? What age?"

Galbatt had absolutely no idea how to gauge the age of a living child, although she could tell the age of a dead one from no more than a kneecap.

She waved her hand at the height the boy had come to, "This big," she said.

"Ah, no, they're all about this big," Perkins laughed, waving his arm a half foot lower than hers.

He saw that she was unsmiling and coughed awkwardly. "All the boys are seven or eight. Once they've hit ten the villagers won't let them come out, they've got their own chores."

Galblatt huffed. "Might have been eight, seemed much older and anyway, he was sitting by the fire. Don't we have a tent for them?"

Perkins scratched his head, "That's odd, mum, we do—" he gestured south, "that way."

Galblatt turned without another word and, from the edge of her tent said, "Goodnight, Perkins."

"Goodnight, Doctor."

Marietta Galblatt sat gingerly on the hammock in her ember-lit tent. What a strange trick of the light, those noodle-fingers.

23, 28. 23, 28. Ages? Times? 1923? 1928? 1923, Carter enters the Tutankhamen tomb. The Roman ruins at Wroxeter in Shropshire are excavated. First dinosaur egg—Andrews in Mongolia. First Tanager expedition. 1928? Penicillin, Griffith's Experiment substantiates DNA, Dunand excavates the Byblos spatula. Ugarit is unearthed. Year 23 AD: nothing. Year 23 BC: nothing. 23000 BC: nothing.

Galblatt tore through the names and dates in her memory, searching for anyone born or deceased those years, any important event. Perhaps they weren't years and anyway, why would an Egyptian kid, whose schools probably didn't even teach Western history, be cryptically referencing the Wroxeter dates?

23: the ninth prime, number of human sex chromosomes, the atomic number of Vanadium. Vanadium. Random. Galblatt couldn't think of a single important use for or product of Vanadium, it wasn't even measurable in most of the fossils and specimens she dealt with.

28: second perfect number. Not a prime. Nickel. Nickel? Galblatt lay back and stared at the ceiling. The average length of a menstrual cycle: 28 days. The time it takes for concrete to dry: 28 days.

2328? What was happening in 2328 BC: Humanity is still sitting in the Indus Valley, Akkadian Empire. Sixth Dynasty of Egypt.

The sequence: 2. 3. 2. 8. Twice the first, halved minus one. No, no sequence.

Galblatt scribbled the numbers on a journal page, rolled over in the hammock, and fell asleep at once.

That night Marietta Galblatt dreamed of spaghetti. Piles of spaghetti, noodles stretching out into the distance as far as the eye could see. She knew she was standing on the brink of evolution. Primordial earth was raging and broiling all around her. Only everything was made of noodles. Noodle mountains rose in the distance, a noodle ocean swept noodle waves up onto the noodle shore. Noodles coiled around her boots, they waved around her legs and in the distance, noodle trees sprouted noodle leaves and a speckling of noodle fungus. Then a noodle cloud descended from the noodle sky toward the shore. Marietta followed it, running through the noodle, her boots squishing beneath her. A meatball rolled casually out of the noodle ocean and came to rest on the noodle shore. The huge noodle in the sky reached toward the meatball, and spaghetti sauce spilled down upon it. Marietta woke up, sweating, in her tent. She made a strong cup of tea and lit a lamp.

The next day was stressful. The camera crew on loan from a film studio in Cairo while the National Geographic's people went back to cut and edit the first three episodes of a "Finding the Bible" holiday special, slipped into an underground cavern, the entrance of which Galblatt's team was just beginning to excavate. They damaged the stonework, the floor, and the ceiling and while trying to extricate themselves, decimated three of their six cameras and two mic booms.

Galblatt spent the morning yelling herself hoarse at the film crew, at the understudy who had laid the tape around the site, and at anyone who would come close enough.

During mid-afternoon break, Galblatt called over all of the village boys and stared them each in the face until they cried. Exercising this sort of power made her feel a little less miserable, but not finding the boy she'd caught in her tent just brought back all of her banished frustration with the numbers 23 and 28.

That afternoon as she was making the rounds to all of the excavation sites within the perimeter, Galblatt overheard a graduate student dictating notes. "At 23 north by 18 minutes 47.75 seconds, 30 east by 3 minutes 57 seconds."

Galblatt paused.

"You," she said to the boy who was taking the dictation, snatching him up by the collar of his shirt. He scrambled out of the hole and inclined his head.

"Yes, Doctor?"

"Let me see your notes." His hand trembled anxiously as he extended the notes he had just taken down.

"We're just south of the city, historically, although with tectonic shift, we may be right on top of the site…" continued the student in the hole. The boy looked anxiously at the notebook.

Galblatt leafed through it until she found the coordinates. "23 degrees," she muttered.

The graduate poked his head out of the hole. "Excuse me, Dr. Galblatt, I didn't know you were here. Do you want to see the progress?"

Galblatt huffed and shoved the notebook back into the waiting hands of the undergrad.

"Go on, then," she said gruffly, waving her hand.

The grad student began rattling off the progress they had made in inches and his own speculations about the site, which had probably once been the food cellar of a house. Galblatt knew that grad students enjoyed this immensely, and listened patiently, not taking in a word of what he was saying. She was thinking about plotting 23 by 28 in her tent, she was sure that was somewhere in the desert, a little south of where they were now, miles from anything. Maybe another site.

"Excellent work, there, keep it up. You better put in a platform if you get anything under four feet. Don't want someone putting a foot through a jar."

The student beamed proudly.

Galblatt preferred working with students to other professionals. When they were dispersed like this, Galblatt always took her pick of students first and let the other archaeologists have the majority of the professionals. The other archaeologists on the site were about fourteen miles away outside of Mut, Egypt with a team of forty-five. Galblatt found she had more control over the dig when her subordinates were groveling at her feet for grants and scholarships, rather than obsessing about their own careers and conducting petty schemes to work on the best digs.

Galblatt had found, in her forty years in the field, that archaeologists were some of the vainest and most dangerous people in existence.

She stepped away from the student and wound her way back through the various patches of indented ground. The sponsors of the expedition had them excavating what was believed to be a small ascetic settlement of around the third century, such as the one that may have been home to Saint Anthony. It was certainly Persian, pre-Muslim, but more likely an Alexandrian village on the trade route. The time was right for ascetics, but the deep rooms, the small amount of artifacts, the huge stable being excavated by Perkin's team, pointed to a trade-route settlement, not a religious settlement.

And even if it was religious, the chances that it had any relation to Saint Anthony, an almost completely fictional character, were astronomical. The people funding a huge portion of the excavation were preying on the inanity of their viewers. Galblatt had trouble understanding why people who were purported to believe that faith requires no substantiation would fork out so much money to substantiate their faith. During her illness, people urged and demanded that she pray— take solace in god. Even doctors, educated men who shouldn't have subscribed to such tripe, told her that her recovery was "in God's hands." But Galblatt never succumbed to the futile and honestly tragic worship of an imaginary deity. When the President died, Galblatt moved through what she knew to be natural, logical and not unimportant stages of grief. But none of these included self-delusion. In a world of science, mathematics, and reason, religion had no real application.

Some years ago, Galblatt had been suspended from a site for inciting aggressive behavior when she encouraged her students to call the sponsor's "Search for the Word" project dangerously childish and naïve on camera. After this experience, declaring that the archeology field was becoming more and more puritanical, Galblatt had trained herself to be more reserved. She was opposed to illogical behavior, fundamentally, so she couldn't help slipping up and rolling her eyes at the television crews and their ludicrously earnest hosts crawling into pre-Egyptian burial caverns saying: "Noah's Ark is likely preserved in a mound of earth such as this."

Codswallop.

She was presently on bad terms with the administration of the college for this offence.

Galblatt finished her rounds at a jog, glancing disinterestedly into the partitioned squares around the main foundation, and returned to her tent. She untied the dusty tent flaps and let them fall together behind her, blocking out the harsh sun.

It was musty and stiflingly hot inside the tent. She went to the wooden chest in the corner and withdrew a battered map of the area. Galblatt preferred the paper maps; she had literally hundreds of every site she had ever excavated. She also had computerized maps and GPS-enabled charting equipment, but the computers failed to conjure up an actual image of a place where people lived. Half of an archaeologist's work was intuition of human behavior and if Galblatt couldn't imagine humans behaving in a place, she couldn't tell people where to dig.

She followed a line down from the top of the map and pressed her forefinger into the exact point of intersection between longitude 23 and latitude 28.

The point was only twenty miles from the camp.

"Boy!" she yelled loudly. A wiry little boy the color of an Anjou pear appeared at her elbow instantly. "Get me a camel."

Loping across the hot desert sand, Marietta Galblatt cursed the domestication of the camel. What a terrifically odorous, useless beast. The camel snorted and spat as if it knew exactly what she was thinking. Its keening moan was like the death cry of a falling albatross.

Galblatt's request for an expedition party had been denied. Actually, the curator (visiting from Mut) had laughed in her face and turned his back without response. Galblatt had taken this as a rejection. She considered hijacking a pair of young boys but feared the talk. Well, she had reasoned, they couldn't punish her for taking *herself* forty-seven miles into the desert.

The air was barely cool enough to breathe. Everything that touched her skin burned her: a flap of cloth, a bit of sand, the prickly-feathered end of her sun-bleached ponytail.

Around midday the camel began to make dying sounds. "What is wrong with you!" Galblatt screamed as the animal bowed underneath her. The ground rushed up and she wriggled free before the camel could topple over onto her. She scuttled across the scalding sand as the animal leaned dangerously, swayed, righted itself, and fell. Even from its knees, the fall was a substantial distance. Dust and sand billowed out from its massive, ugly body. "A faulty animal!" Galblatt screamed again, "Gave me a faulty animal." But there was no one there to hear her. She was a good four hours from the camp, so much farther from actual civilization.

Galblatt sat for a while. The sand directly beneath her was cool, everything else burned. The heat waves off the desert sand were making her seasick. She stared. No, it wasn't heat waves. Something was twisting around on the horizon. It was a long, fleshy finger. It was beckoning.

Galblatt blinked, closed her eyes. The finger was projected in reverse on the hot pink insides of her eyelids. Beckon. Beckon.

She opened her eyes again and it was still beckoning. It was more definite now, a finger, a long, flat finger. Like a noodle, wobbly and flaccid, waving around on the horizon. But it ended in heat waves. She couldn't see where it connected to a hand, or an arm, or a body.

She was relatively sure she was hallucinating. She tried to ignore it. She pulled her tent out from under the camel and draped it over her, thinking she'd sleep until night and then walk back to camp in the dark. There was no way she was getting there in the middle of the day. Best to sleep through the heat.

Years ago, Marietta had wandered off into the desert, out of the camp. She remembered the dizzying panic when she was out of sight of the camp and completely directionless. She had stormed off after an argument with the President and, in an area almost identical to this, she'd finally stopped walking and realized she had no idea where she was. There had been a long hill which seemed to wave back and forth. It wasn't a dune, it had a structure beneath the sand, rock or an old section of a fallen wall. The actual placement of the sun was impossible to discern, the whole sky was a blinding whiteness. She was dehydrated, and the complete silence pressed in on her. No wind, no insects, no sand tinkling over sand. Silence.

She walked up to the top of the hill and collapsed. Under the burning sand, in Marietta's dreams, a huge twisting arm had lain, petrified, the once soft, rounded arm of some squid-like creature of incomprehensible proportions. In her dreams, the handless arm curled around her, cradling her like an infant as she slept, and when she woke, night had fallen and the only interruption of the clearest, fullest, most intense night sky of her entire life was the blur of firelight in the west: the camp. The arm seemed to point toward it, toward the President, asleep in his tent. And by the time Marietta stumbled back into the camp, ragged and blistered by the sun the President, from the back of a camel, was radioing a helicopter to search the perimeter, preparing to embark himself on a rescue mission to find her. It was dawn and the sky was pink. And she loved him.

Galblatt awoke. The change in temperature had been rousing her for a long time. Her eyelids snapped open. She could feel the heat from the earth, but no heat from the sky. She threw off the tent and took a look at the camel. Still dead.

But on the horizon was a light. The weird thoughts of the first expedition with the President must have affected her brain. There was no way she was still within sight of the camp. She checked the compass. And, indeed, if she had started out in the right direction, the light was in the opposite direction of the camp.

Galblatt paused. At best, it was another dig site, preferably of some nationality whose language she spoke. Hopefully at 23, 28. At worst... what? Who else would be out here? Thieves? Pirates?

What were the chances of that?

Probably some nomadic tribe with water, food, and transportation. Galblatt never kept local currency on her, but they might trade for the tent, for canteens, for the camel's carpet. She quickly stripped the animal, tied everything she could up in a pack and slung it over her back.

The light was not far off, maybe three hours, or four. She quickened her pace. The pack cut into her shoulders.

The ground was well-lit by the stars, everything was pale blue. After an hour she was making good time. The light was burning hugely, bigger than a fire. It must have been a city, but what city was out here, in the middle of the Sahara… almost literally?

Not a city that Galblatt knew of. Not a city with a telephone.

She kept walking. The straps of the pack bent her shoulders forward. Sweat trickling down her arms felt like icy fingers stroking her flesh. Her knees kept buckling beneath her, plunging her into the sand. Thirst and muscle fatigue made her shiver. Eventually the light was bright enough that Galblatt should have been able to distinguish houses or tents but there was nothing except wide, soft tendrils of light, emanating from what looked like a single, tall, jagged dune against an otherwise gently rolling horizon.

Blinded by the bright light, she crawled across the sand toward the mountain.

It was porous… like a knot of tree roots covered in plastic.

And then Marietta Galblatt realized what she was looking at. And the sun was paling the eastern sky. And she realized how long she must have been traveling. That she was at 23, 28.

It was a monstrous pile of spaghetti. Each waving noodle was iridescent with light.

Galblatt hoisted herself up off the sand and dropped the heavy pack she had dragged across the desert to this spaghetti mountain. She was struck by the pointlessness of having brought it along. And she took a final step toward the mountain.

A noodle shot toward her and seemed to prod her in the chest with its huge tentacle. This, surely, was the reason she had been called to 23, 28. The reason she had been visited by the noodle boy, the reason she had argued with the curator. The reason she had been able to hike these twenty miles into the desert on foot. She felt her chest expand with pride and happiness.

The noodle shape seemed to rise as well. Galblatt thought of her frenzied description to the President of the mound she had slept on in the desert. She remembered the beads of sweat breaking over her eyebrows as she tried feverishly to plot exactly where she had been. Faithful, believing, the President had sent out parties, had sent out the rescue helicopter to look at the area. The chances of finding anything in the untraveled waste of the desert, where no one went but pirates and those horrendous nomadic people, all twisted into leprous shapes as they pulled themselves through the barren landscape, were impossible. Any hint was worth investigation. But Galblatt took the effort as a pledge of affection.

The President's assistants told her, pulling her roughly aside, that he was not interested in her, but what she might have found in a sun-drunk stupor. He had not been going out to save her, but to save the college a tremendous lawsuit.

Their words rolled off her. They found nothing. There was nothing in the radius she may have traveled from the camp. She had hallucinated, misjudged, let him down, let them all down.

But here. Here, at 23, 28, she was standing on the shape, that sand-backed, dome-topped wall she was so sure she had seen. The noodle that had prodded her withdrew into its roiling mass of light shapes. Galblatt squinted, trying to make out the texture of the rock face that supported this massive dune. It was not a wall, but an actual dome. It was completely round. Sand was shifting off the sides, the massive noodle creature's weight was unearthing the structure. It was an almost perfect sphere, pockmarked, like a meatball. A petrified meatball.

Galblatt tumbled backward off the now bare structure and landed, face-down, in the rough sand. The light dimmed. The creature was gone.

She could hear the sounds of scraping metal and laughter. The light disappeared, leaving Galblatt sun-blinded, blinking back tears of surprise and exhaustion. Her sunburnt eyelids crinkled painfully. Real lights, the lights of gas lamps, were shining around her. A generator was humming coolly some ways away and the laughter, sounding more and more familiar, was coming from a glowing white tent surrounded by a cluster of smaller, rattier tents. A large mismatched herd of camels, horses and some out-of-place-looking mules were tied outside the cluster of tents. Some were standing, some kneeling on the ground. Galblatt felt a twinge of annoyance and regret, remembering the camel that had been sacrificed to bring her here. But where was here?

Galblatt moved toward the camels. They grunted and bayed in annoyance at her approach. Packs of supplies littered the ground around them. Some still bore their ragged saddles and trappings. Galblatt lifted the flap of a bag. Guns. Three semi-automatics and a nest of pistols. Another bag, guns. Guns, guns, dried meat of some sort, a large cache of passports, wallets, two thick wads of American one-hundred-dollar bills, what looked like a tool set, and guns.

Terrorists? Bandits? Galblatt whirled around, a jolt of fear interrupting the feeling of peace which had settled on her since the encounter with the noodle creature. She briefly contemplated pocketing one of the wads of bills, for bartering purposes. But, considering all of the guns, she decided against it. The laughter rolled out of the tent again. It was familiar, distinctively familiar, laughter.

She crept into the cluster of tents.

"Now that he's dead," someone said. Galblatt strained her ears, pressing up against a tent not far from the larger, lighted white tent in the center. They were speaking English, these people. They were pirates. Desert pirates.

"What we'll need," a man said, "What we'll need is someone who knows their way around the camps. We need someone who knows how to take charge, a... you know... a leader."

"That's right, someone to keep these people in line. Someone organized."

"Pass the rum, captain," said another, "Argh."

That laughter again. It was dawn and the sky was pink. And Galblatt knew, quite suddenly, that the laughter belonged to the President.

And she cleared her throat outside the door of the tent.

SAY THANKS

by Andersen Prunty

My mother sat at the kitchen table, smoke from her cigarette curling around her head. She stared vacantly at an invisible spot just in front of her.

"You need to go upstairs and look in the bedroom," she said. "And remember to be thankful."

I was going to question her but that part about being thankful sounded good. It wasn't my birthday or Mega Buffet Day but I wasn't going to quibble. I went upstairs and into my parents' bedroom, wondering what the surprise could possibly be.

My father lay face down on the floor.

"Dad?" I said.

I walked toward him. I was going to reach down and nudge him but what if he...

"He's dead." Mom appeared in the doorway.

"How did it..."

"That's not important. The important thing is that it was meant to happen and we should thank the Monster."

"But I don't believe in..."

She had moved next to me and now quickly silenced me with a finger over my lips.

"We don't talk like that in this house. You're going to help me with the ceremonies, aren't you?"

"I'll help however you want me to."

"Besides, we hadn't really gotten along for a while. I'm pretty sure we were headed for a divorce. He drank all the time and sometimes he hit me. He may have been having an affair. Of course, I'll have to start masturbating again. Sex was really the only thing I got from him. You masturbate, don't you, Charlie?"

I slowly nod my head, still trying to digest the death of my father.

"Of course, I'm female so it means masturbation is even better. Did you know a woman can have two types of orgasms?"

"I never really thought about it."

"It's true. You've got the clitoris near the outside, and that one can send you through the roof. But then you've got your G-spot way back in there. It varies from woman to woman. Hit this the right way and you can have a really long, deep orgasm. Of course I don't really mean *you*. You don't have a vagina. That was one of the things I liked about your father though. When we coupled, the head of his penis hit my G-spot perfectly and it felt like I came the whole time. I'll probably have to buy a dildo. Ready to get his clothes off?"

I was well-familiar with the ritual. We stripped off his clothes and took him down to the car. He was too stiff to fit in the backseat so we had to fasten him to the roof with cables.

Mom told me she was too upset to drive to the dump so I did.

"Now that your father's gone, I'll probably lose everything. You understand that, don't you? I haven't worked a day in my life and we... I mean, *I* still owe on the car and the house. I'll probably have to move into your apartment. But if that happens it was meant to be. The Monster has a plan for each of us." She looked west, toward Ristorante Familia. She spent the rest of the trip calling family members.

We reached the dump and drove around the lot until we found the corpse pile.

Mom slid her phone back in her purse and said, "Well, Aunt Carla's not coming. Bitch."

I honked the horn to clear somebody else's grieving family members and pulled up to the pile of corpses. It looked like it had been a busy week.

I got out of the car and looked at the bodies, all in various states of decay, all traditionally nude.

"All this sadness," I said.

"All this joy," Mom said. "Each of these bodies represents a joyful life lived on earth and an eternal life after. When our time comes, when we're stripped naked and taken to the dump, we'll see your father again. I'll hopefully have remarried by the time that happens."

I didn't really believe her. It still seemed overwhelmingly sad to me. I tried to keep myself from crying but a small sob and maybe a tear or two escaped.

Mom looked over at me. "You better bottle that shit up. Keep it all in there. Nobody wants to be around your negativity and pessimism. You're going to have the loneliest funeral ever."

I moved the car out of the way and waited for the other family members to arrive. Our family was small and insular, mostly ignorant and afraid of outsiders, so there weren't that many people there. We stared at the pile of corpses and exchanged stories about my dad. It was hard to find positive things to say about him so we just decided to laugh a lot as we told about finding him passed out, picking him up from the police station, discovering missing objects and money, nursing our wounds. The laughter added a layer of respectful levity. Or maybe, to an outsider, a kind of frenzied madness.

When we got bored Mom finally said, "May the Flying Spaghetti Monster bless his soul," and we all went to Ristorante Familia.

We sat around a large table presided over by Father Vincent Severity. He didn't really say much. Mostly he only spoke to relay a bawdy story from his soldiering days or to have a violent outburst directed at a member of the wait staff. We all had the same thing—a plate of spaghetti covered in marinara sauce and two meatballs. We couldn't begin eating until Severity blessed the food.

"Today is another celebration of the Flying Spaghetti Monster's awesome generosity. It is not just that He has reclaimed the life of Peter Thorazine, it is that He welcomes Peter Thorazine into the afterlife. So we will partake of the Flying Spaghetti Monster—the pasta of his flesh, the sauce of his blood, the meatballs of his dual brain. Amen."

We were all ravenous and ate quickly. A server took all the empty plates away and brought us buckets. We all vomited into the buckets to symbolize the rebirth of the Monster. Then we all went out to try and find unfortunate hungry people to partake of the vomit, as a symbol of the Monster's generosity.

It was dark by the time I got Mom home. I didn't know how she was doing and I didn't really care.

"Well, see you next week," I said.

"You don't need to bother coming over. I'll probably be trolling the bars looking for a new husband. If it's the Monster's will..."

"Whatever."

"All right. I'm going to go inside and masturbate now."

She got out of the car and I drove away before she even made it onto the porch. I turned on the radio and figured Mom must have messed with the settings. It was a Monster rock station where the singer just sings about the Monster instead of a girl. It sounded creepy and strange. I scanned the stations until I found something that didn't have any words at all. I thought about getting something to eat because I was starving but tradition dictated eating nothing but the ceremonial dinner until the following day. I drove back to my tiny room in the ghetto and tried to fall asleep amidst the hunger and the sounds of people fucking and fighting. I heard gunshots and thought to myself how that was just another example of the Monster's generosity. I put my hands over my growling stomach and thought about all the things I was thankful for.

THE NOODLY APPENDAGE THAT FEEDS YOU

by Kirk Jones

He was alone. The last pirate stripper had died nearly a week ago and their ship, now his ship, was at least thirty days from shore. Barney feared he would never see land again. The only consolation was that the last body he had consumed actually tasted pleasant in comparison to the others, and, together with the many herbs and spices aboard, produced an exquisite stockpile of meatballs.

They were now all but depleted. He plucked the last stripperball from storage and savored it as much as near starvation would allow. His stomach rumbled like thunder on the distant horizon as night drew close.

Those few remaining on the planet acquainted with Darwin's theory of evolution would have bemoaned Barney's survival over the others aboard the Ziti. It was brazen hunger that had led to his survival, nothing more. The others were as strong of will as they were of flesh, and they refused to eat their comrades upon their untimely deaths. Barney, on the other hand, remained shameless, feasting upon the flesh of his dead brethren until their bones were stripped clean. Then he left their remains to bleach in the sun, attempting to lure any birds of prey who might pass by. Of course, being thirty days from land, there was no hope of this happening, but Barney remained optimistic until that last stripperball passed through his jaws and into his sizable gullet.

He grasped the mass of flesh sagging at his midriff. Though it was ample enough to weigh him down considerably, it no longer hung below his genitals, and he knew that the end was nigh. The only option remaining was to suck the marrow from his shipmates' bones, which at best would give him a few more days.

Two hours later the bones had been shattered and Barney rested at the center of the ship, staring into the stars above. He had eaten everything his crew members left for him. The only sustenance remaining on the ship sat in three barrels below deck, which contained between them nearly twenty pounds of spaghetti.

Captain Pici had made it clear before departure that nobody was to eat the sacred pasta. It was to be distributed to the natives of a distant continent, as a test of sorts. Those who beheld the spaghetti with a sense of wonder were to be indoctrinated accordingly. Those who ate it were to be shot on sight. For those aboard the ship, eating the noodles before arrival would mean execution. Not eating the noodles would likely result in a quicker, more temperate death by starvation if things went awry.

Things had gone terribly awry, and Barney decided that since everyone else aboard the vessel was dead he would eat the pasta. But as he opened the first barrel of al dente, capellini pasta, he hesitated. He beheld in that barrel his lord and savior, or the earthly manifestation of his lord and savior at the least.

He contemplated then, as he tested the pasta for firmness, the true nature of his holiness. If he were to manifest, would he manifest as an al dente, or an overcooked variety?

Barney determined that his God would be overcooked, so

that he could bend and weave through all things. Since the first barrel of pasta was not an accurate reflection of his lord's graven image, Barney decided to eat it.

The next morning Barney awoke to find the first barrel empty. He had eaten to the point of incapacitation and continued in a blackout frenzy until the entire barrel was gone. And he was getting hungry again, so he opened the next barrel of pasta. Inside he found overcooked capellini. This led Barney to reflect further upon the true nature of his God. Sure, he would most definitely be overcooked, logic permitted no other option. But would his God be capellini, or of a thicker diameter?

Barney decided the spaghetti monster would most definitely be of wider diameter than capellini, and if he was too firm he would likely break. His noodly holiness would be spaghettoni, a large-noodled God. This barrel too would make a fine meal, Barney concluded, because it also was not an accurate representation of his God.

The second barrel of pasta took the edge off Barney's hunger, but he could still feel starvation nipping at his heels. Reluctantly, he cracked the third barrel to reveal overcooked spaghettoni. No, the pasta was thicker than spaghettoni. It was the thickest noodle Barney had ever laid eyes upon. Truly, this was an accurate reflection of his holiness.

He decided then and there not to eat the pasta in the third barrel. This was a test to determine his adherence to the holy commandments. To eat the pasta would be to defecate upon all that was sacred. And while he had wiped himself once as a young boy in the monastery with several pages of the Pastafarian scripture when he ran out of toilet paper, to defecate directly onto the holy laws, whether literally or metaphorically, was unacceptable.

He locked himself in a nearby room and prayed for the spaghetti monster to redeem him, to lock the door from the outside so that he could not eat when hunger called to him.

His lord did not answer.

Finally, he left the room, rolled the barrel to the deck, and dropped it into the water below. As it plunged into the murky depths, Barney realized the mistake he had made. In retrospect, he was not sure if it was his stomach, or his guilt which made him decide to jump overboard. In either event, his impulse overrode logic—as his weight overrode his grip on the floating barrel—and he sank into the ocean.

He clawed at the surface to no avail, until a bright light engulfed him and he was plucked from the water and drawn into the heavens by a noodly appendage. When he finally arrived at his unknown destination, he saw before him the revered spaghetti monster. It spoke not with words, but by constricting a thick mass of noodles around its meatball eyes. "Barney, you are not meant to die yet."

Barney bowed before the revered spaghetti monster. "I ran out of food. I would have starved before reaching land."

The spaghetti monster cradled Barney. His doughy tentacle-like digits were just as Barney had imagined, soft and thick. "I gave you three barrels of pasta. If you weren't such a goddamned glutton you could have stretched it for thirty days."

"Forgive me, lord."

"I will do more than that," the spaghetti monster gurgled. "I will restore you, and set you upon your boat. When you arrive at your destination, I want you to bear witness. Let the people know that I am a merciful God, one whose pleasure stems from my subjects' culinary indulgences. Let them eat pasta."

"Yes, my lord."

Barney closed his eyes until the blinding light was replaced by the calm, redundant crashing of waves against his ship. As proof of his vision, the spaghetti monster had also restored the final barrel of pasta. Barney dutifully counted the individual strands, and limited himself to six strands of pasta a day for the next three weeks until land was in sight.

As the shore drew closer, Barney was overwhelmed by a sense of familiarity. The city in the distance looked just like his home. Much to his surprise, the new world was civilized.

When he arrived in the docks, he lowered the anchor into the waters and waited for the boat to stop. The men ashore called to their brethren in Barney's native language, beckoning them to assist those aboard. Barney knew then that it was his God's will that he be returned home, to bear witness for his own people.

When they boarded, they found only Barney, perched against the rear mast, the last strands of pasta dangling from his mouth. "Friends, I saw him! Our God!" He walked toward them, arms outstretched, stumbling over the bones of his comrades. "He wants us to savor him! He wants us to eat!" Barney pushed the noodles hanging from his chin into his mouth and chewed. "Join me!" he cried.

"Treason!" One of the onlookers shouted.

"He's killed the crew!"

Before Barney could utter another word, the men drew their swords and gutted him.

"Wait," he said, "our lord... asked me to tell you."

His words were cut short as the men pried his mouth open, trying to salvage what little pasta remained in tact in his throat.

As his insides spilled onto the floorboards now awash with his blood, Barney smiled, knowing that, even though the spaghetti monster's decree had been carried out in vain, he had done as commanded. And though his brethren had forsaken him for eating the noodly appendage that fed him spiritually for years, he had felt the warm embrace of spaghettoni and lived for a short time to tell about it.

He thought he felt that appendage again now, encompassing

his neck, cradling him, drawing him up into the air. And as the men continued to hack away at his suspended remains, he imagined his legs as meatballs, and his intestines as thick, overcooked strands of pasta. He envisioned himself an earthly manifestation of his lord, and knew that if he could partake, he would make a fine meal indeed.

PRAISE THE LORD AND PASS THE PARMESAN

by Steve Lowe

I was certain the dark red liquid dripping from my fingers and pooled all around me was my own blood, and that I was dead. The face of the Lord floated above me, beckoning. His large, round eyes, perched above his head like alien antennae, looked down upon me lovingly, and I felt no fear. It was quite the opposite in fact. To finally know for certain that God did exist, and that in the hour of my death, He had come for me, was most comforting. His long, drooping arms opened wide, ready to fold me in and welcome me Home.

I reached out my hand to Him and rivulets of blood ran down my arm, gathered at my elbow, dripped onto my T-shirt. The carnage of my living body did not frighten me, either. What had been done to me in life was no longer of consequence. I laughed at the evil in the world, that which would tear my flesh to the bone and leave me here for dead. What evil could possibly come to me now, for I am saved?

"I knew you were real, Father."

I closed my eyes and his heavenly breath flowed over me. "Good to see you, Donnie." It was as though an oven had opened and the scent of fresh garlic bread wafted out. My stomach growled in response. Heaven smelled fantastic!

"Is this heaven, Father?"

"This is Nebraska, Donnie."

"Heaven is in Nebraska, Father?"

"No, Donnie, you're not in heaven. You're still in Nebraska."

I was confused and I brought my fingers to my lips. I inhaled the scent of my own blood, my flesh come undone in the hour of my ascendency into His Heavenly Fold. It smelled delicious, a mixture of tomato and garlic and basil. Possibly some rosemary in there, as well. I sniffed again. Yes, definitely a pinch of rosemary, and it must be fresh. That was a nice touch. You don't often find fresh rosemary in the mangled flesh of the dead.

"How did I get to Nebraska, Father?"

"Donnie, you *live* in Nebraska. And stop calling me Father, it's weird."

"But aren't you the Father of all creation, Father? Didn't you construct me from the dust on the ground, in your image? I would think that technically qualifies you as my father, even if normal intercourse and impregnation of a female weren't actually involved."

"OK, yes, technically, I'm the father. Can you do me a favor and open your eyes so we can have a normal conversation?"

I did as the Lord bade me do. He was difficult to look upon, floating in the air above me, backlit by fantastic rays of golden sunlight, adding shadows and contours to His glorious noodly appendages. They dripped with the sweet nectar of life, plopping down on my face, splattering my clothes. His holy juices touched my lips and I flicked out my tongue to taste God. He was scrumptious! Only the best sun-dried tomatoes, enough garlic that you knew it was there, but not so much that it overwhelmed the flavors of the onion and perfectly proportioned herbs. I noted the rosemary, twittering upon my tongue like a ballerina and dancing as it slid down my gullet. I lapped up the Lord, savoring His saucey goodness.

"Donnie, stop that!"

I opened my eyes, slightly drunk from His holy ambrosia and craving a piece of that garlic bread I smelled earlier. "Stop what, Father?"

"Stop licking your arm, you dumbass."

"But you're delicious, oh Host of Hosts."

That's when the Lord reached out and slapped me across the face. It was a sharp, stinging blow that splattered tomato sauce in my eyes and left an angry noodle-shaped welt on my cheek. And that's also when I saw the Lord for the first time for what He really is.

"Father..." I didn't know what else to say to Him, aside from the urge to request some grated Parmesan.

"What is it, Donnie? I'm busy, you know."

"Yes, I'm sorry. I was just wondering why you are here."

"Because you called out my name."

"I did?"

He pointed a slender Angel Hair arm and said, "Yes, last night. You don't remember?"

I looked to the spot where he was pointing and noticed the girl for the first time. I was in my room, lying in my bed next to a young woman I had almost no recollection of, aside from vague, besotted fumblings in the dark. "Oh, right. I must have forgotten about... Melissa. Or maybe it's Miranda." I chalked up my cloudy recollection to being in the presence of His Holy Pasta. "But, why now, oh Lord? I've called to you before, but you never made an appearance."

He dug a noodle into His glorious midsection, rooted around for a moment, and produced a can of Natural Light. "Like I said, I'm busy. And besides, you probably weren't ready to see me until now."

He swilled the can of beer through a writhing orifice of sauce-laden pasta. When he was done, he belched, a wave of malty Italian breath washing over me. I rubbed my skin, trying to absorb His glorious regurgitation.

"So, look, I got this thing with this guy pretty soon. I should probably go now."

"Wait, Lord." I rose to my knees and clasped my hands before me, prayerful and subservient before the Holy Pasta. "Please, tell me what I should do next. What is your plan for my life?"

He looked down at a bare noodle arm and said, "Yeah, that'll take a while, and oh! Look at the time. I'm running late. Best if you just go to services every Friday. Lots of answers there."

"OK, thank you Father."

"Later, dude."

He vanished from my sight, as if he had never been there at all. The blood that had covered my body, not blood at all but tasty drippings from His Worshipfulness, was gone as well. I wasn't dead at all. I didn't even appear to be slightly injured. I might have thought myself a crazy man, and the floating pile of spaghetti that spoke to me as the Lord God a simple hallucination, had I not still smelled garlic in the air, and tasted sauce on my lips. I shoved my bedmate's rump until she began to stir.

"Miranda, wake up."

"My name's not Miranda, it's Melinda," she said in a thick, groggy, hung over voice.

"I've had an awakening."

"Well congratulations, now I have too." She ran a hand through her tousled hair and yawned. It filled me with a passion unlike that which coursed through my veins just the night before. No longer did I desire this woman in such a way. My days of fornication stopped then, and I knew I had much work to do to walk the path of God. I must make an honest woman of this girl, and she an honest man of me.

"We must consummate our relationship, for I have seen the face of God, and this sinful life of mine shall go on no longer."

"We already did some consummating, unless you don't remember last night."

She wasn't understanding me. I tried to clarify my noble intentions. "Melissa, we must put our relationship right in the eyes of the Lord." I slid off the bed, dropped to one knee and clasped her gentle though slightly wrinkled hand in mine; tenderly caressing the hard callouses on her palm caused by years of spinning around a shiny pole.

"Will you marry me?"

She didn't marry me, so I had to attend my first church service alone that Friday night. The greeter at the door was very pleased to see me, and spoke the words of the Lord unto me, filling my mortal coil with great joy.

"Welcome to Olive Garden, just one tonight?"

"Dear sister, there can never be just one. With God in my heart, I'll always have room for two. Maybe three if I get married someday, and as much as five should the Lord bless us with the gift of new life."

She ogled me, no doubt overcome by the powerful light of God I radiated unto her. I looked down at her hand and, observing that her ring finger bore no mark of prior betrothing, let His will guide me to my new purpose.

"Um, so… you need a table for two then?" she said.

I dropped to a knee and read her nametag. "Carrie, my beloved, I have so much to give. Will you do the honor of marrying me so that we might spread His word together for eternity?"

"Hey Kyle, there's a weird guy out here!"

I grabbed for her hand, but she pulled away, clearly too shy to accept my offer until this Kyle arrived to witness for us. I swelled with pride at her quick, practical thinking. We would make a superb couple.

"Excuse me, sir. May I help you with something?"

This man's nametag read Kyle and I beamed at him. He must've been a church elder, and now that we were official, our courtship could proceed.

"Kyle, this guy is totally trying to hit on me."

Kyle stepped between my soon-to-be bride and myself and spoke politely, "Sir, could you please stand up?" He turned around and motioned my love away as I returned to my upright and locked position.

"Ah, you are wise," I said. "Better to institute a waiting period prior to the official betrothing, lest she become overwhelmed with emotion and unable to properly accept. They do this when buying handguns as well, you know."

"Sir, I'm going to have to ask you to leave. You're frightening the staff and driving away customers."

"I see." I didn't see, but it seemed to be a good thing to say. "Perhaps then you could direct me to a pew before the service begins."

Kyle's eyes became very narrow and I thought perhaps he was having trouble seeing, but he was really just becoming sly. "Services? What services are you talking about?"

I too attempted to be sly and whispered from the side of my mouth, "You know, od-Gay?"

This only confused poor Kyle, who seemed to be somewhat dense for a church elder. "What the hell is od-Gay?"

Perhaps he was just an assistant to the elder, and therefore unfamiliar with my ancient Latin phrasing. "God. I'm here for

Friday services to worship God."

"Oh."

"Yeah."

"And, just what does this God of yours look like?"

I was all set to launch into a fervent description of His Holiness, thinking this some sort of test, or secret handshake, to get inside. It made sense when you thought about it. But a young woman garbed in the official church attire walked by at just that moment carrying a stack of plastic-encased church directories to hand out to the newly arriving parishioners. I spirited one away, telling her, "The Lord be with you." I held the directory in front of me, momentarily surprised by the inclusion of what appeared to be mandatory tithing amounts listed next to each entry, and pointed to the grand photo of God in the middle of the handout. It was strange to see Him lying in a dish with two large forks mercilessly plunged into his noodly sides, but then I recalled His crucifixion, and figured this was a recreation of the glorious moment when He gave Himself up for His people. It was a dark time in the history of mankind, referred to in this piece of official church scripture as *The Bottomless Bowl Weekend Celebration!* I had so much to learn.

"This being God?" I said to Kyle as I pointed at the photo.

His eyes grew wide and he looked around conspiratorially. "Yes, I see." He hooked my arm and guided me forward into the labyrinthine halls of God's house. The aroma of pasta and the lighthearted banter of His people filled me with a joy I have never known before, or since. We strolled past the congregation to the rear of the building, where there was much commotion with altar boys and girls running this way and that. I instantly became very excited, for I was certain I knew what was happening next.

"Oh, are you taking me to the baptismal suite?"

Kyle brightened, a great smile spreading across his face.

"Yes, that's *exactly* where I'm taking you." He threw open a door and motioned me toward the back of a small, cold room. "Please, step inside and we will be right with you to begin the service."

"Thank you, brother." The baptismal suite was an amazing room, filled with racks and racks of food boxes and bins loaded with different vegetables. I imagined the glorious feast that this recently trucked-in bounty would become, and hoped that my baptism would be official before it happened. I was just sitting down next to His Holiness at the great banquet table in my mind when the door opened again. Kyle had returned with two altar boys, dressed in dirty white aprons, stained by the good work of the Lord, no doubt. One held a basket of breadsticks and the other a large tureen filled with red sauce. Kyle's infectious grin had spread to his two assistants, and I couldn't help smiling myself. I was bursting with anticipation at what would happen next.

"Good sir, please fall to your knees, clasp your hands behind your back, and close your eyes so that this ceremony may begin."

I did as instructed, trembling from excitement as well as from the chill inside the very cold baptismal suite. God must have given up His body to save his people during the wintertime. The three purveyors of His Holy word stood before me.

"Now, open your mouth," Kyle said.

Once again, I did as instructed.

"And the Lord said, 'Take this, all of you and eat, for this is my body, given up for you.'"

A breadstick filled my mouth entirely. It felt as though Kyle had shoved it in whole until it jabbed at the back of my throat and broke into large chunks that pushed my cheeks out. I choked a bit, but kept my eyes shut and breathed through my nose. There was no way I would defile my very own baptism by gagging on the Lord's body.

"Then the Lord said, 'Take this, all of you and drink, for this is my blood, shed for you.'"

The sauce came next in large glops, flowing over my chin and filling my mouth and nose. I couldn't help but gag this time, but I fought through it valiantly, chewing and swallowing and choking and coughing. As the Holy concoction slid down my throat and burned my sinuses, I could actually feel my body swell with the presence of the Lord. Through this Holy sacrament, that breadstick and tomato sauce had truly transformed into the body and blood of the Lord my God. Tears flowed down my face, first from the near asphyxiation, but then from a truly spiritual transformation as I became saved, a believer, a follower. I was now truly a child of God.

Finally, Kyle said, "And the Lord concluded by saying, 'Take this, all of you, and sleep, for this is my fist, laid down upon thee so that I may relieve you of all the shit in thine pockets.'"

I blacked out when he punched me in the face.

I came to in an alley, lying among refuse in a puddle of liquid that smelled of urine. I'm pretty sure it was my own, as was the blood in my mouth. My wallet was missing, as were two of my front teeth. Apparently, the fist portion of the baptism didn't take at first, and they had to do it over again several times. That would explain why my ribs ached as well, but it did not account for my missing pants.

Oh, this was a low time for me.

As I trudged home in my torn shirt and piddled-in underwear, I tried to understand what had happened. No God would allow such a demeaning, humiliating baptismal procedure. Either Kyle and his altar boys were not familiar with the proper steps, or I'd been had. That must have been it. I got took. Hoodwinked. Bamboozled. Led astray. Run amok. Anger clouded my love. Confusion disrupted my devotion. I climbed into my house through an open window, for my keys had also been lost to the devils of The Olive Garden Church of the Lord. I curled into a ball on my bed and cried out. I screamed at God, demanding He show His starchy face to me once more and explain Himself. But He did not come that night.

I tell you, the Lord works in mysterious ways.

He came to me as before, in the faint light of early morning, though behind him blazed the light of a thousand suns. He woke me by tossing an empty vodka bottle on my head. I was grateful that it was a cheap plastic drugstore brand, and instantly humbled myself before Him, begging forgiveness for taking His name in vain the night before.

"What the hell are you talkin' about, dude?" The Lord sounded tired.

"Lord, what happened last night?"

He laughed and slapped my shoulder with a saucy noodle. "Holy shit, Donnie, what the hell *didn't* happen last night?"

"I mean at church. Did you not see that sham of a baptism?"

He rubbed a noodle against his right meatball and pondered for a moment. "I don't know. Did it involve a redhead, a blonde and a two-foot-long dildo?"

"Heavens, no!"

"Then I didn't see it." He squinted at me for a moment then his eyes grew into huge saucers. "Goddamn, what the hell happened to your face, Holmes?"

"That's what I… should you be taking your own name in vain?" I decided not to wait for that answer and just plunged into my recounting of the church service. God removed a cigar from behind his left meatball and stoked up while I regaled him with every detail of his wayward House of God.

"Those little pricks! Who do they think they are, acting like that in my name?"

"I know, right? That's blasphemous as hell, isn't it?"

"You're damn straight, especially since I ain't seen my cut of anything yet. Those little bastards need to be taught a lesson." He seemed angry, but his mood quickly changed as his face grew long. He stretched and yawned heavily. "But I think that can wait for tomorrow. I need to drag my ass into bed."

"OK, Father. Rest well."

He reached out a noodle, ruffled my hair and said with a slur, "You take it easy little buddy. Say hi to that Melina chick for me, k?"

I didn't have the heart to tell him about Marissa. "Good night, God."

And he was gone. I felt much better. The pain from my baptism thrummed on my face and made breathing difficult, but the discomfort was lessened by the Lord's words. I shuffled to the kitchen to look for some ibuprofen. As I searched the cabinets for a bottle, I heard the front door lock click open. I froze for a moment, frightened, but then I realized that it could only be one person breaking into my house using my own key. I snuck into the hall and peered around the corner, barely able to contain my excitement. It bordered on giddiness, truth be told. The elder known as Kyle eased inside and looked around, careful not to make a sound as he closed the door. No doubt, he had come to gather some extra tithes for the Lord. But I had something else in mind.

As I said, God works in mysterious ways.

Kyle was confused when he woke up. He had no idea what to make of the plastic kiddie pool in which he sat, nor the puddle of spaghetti sauce beneath the chair to which I had tied his naked body. His screams were muffled by the pair of soiled underwear I stuffed down his throat.

"Brother Kyle, good morning to you! Or, I guess, technically it's afternoon now, so good afternoon!"

He was not as pleased to see me as I was to see him. He had been unconscious for many hours from the bowling trophy-shaped lump on his head, and I was growing weary from cooking. Thirteen boxes of pasta noodles and almost three gallons of spaghetti sauce took much longer to cook than I had anticipated. But the hard work was over. Now, it was time to do the Lord's good work.

As I dumped pot after pot of noodles over Kyle, I told him, "I have a message from the Lord. He wanted to deliver it personally, but He's a little busy right now, so I figured I would handle it for Him. You know, it's an incredible sensation, to feel the hand of the Host reach inside you and use you for His glorious good. I am a piece of clay in His hands, and he is the divine sculptor of my life."

Next I used an empty pot to ladle sauce onto Kyle's head. I wanted the sauce to be steaming, just like in the picture from the holy scripture at Kyle's church, but alas, gallons of cooked sauce does not stay warm for long in a kiddie pool, which was as close as I could come to replicating a large serving bowl. But the best part was still to come. Who knew blessed art could be so much fun?

"God said you needed to be taught a lesson. I figured what better lesson than the one He taught to us? As I'm sure you know, being an elder in the house of the Lord and all, our Savior so loved us that he sacrificed Himself. Our God is a great God!"

That sounded right, though I wasn't entirely certain how

that piece of biblical history actually went. I wished I could have at least gotten in one church service. So much still to know, new discoveries to make and lessons to learn! I felt like a Holy sponge, ready to soak up His truth!

The sauce knocked off a lot of the noodles, leaving only a few clinging to his trembling torso. I considered removing the chair and just having him sit in the pool, but then he would probably try to run away, and I couldn't have that before the final touch was added. The last piece of this blessed recreation was still to come.

Kyle messed himself when I pulled the hay forks from behind the couch. I thought there was something poetic to that as I drove them into his sides and said, "Praise the Lord, dinner is served!"

VESICA

by J. David Osborne

The cowboy turned away from the barista, slipped the change into his pocket, and sat down. Women with glittering T-shirts tapped feet. Thick rimmed glasses glossed pages. Art on the walls, computers plugged in, men in collared shirts crossed legs and talked. The cowboy's gums ached for tobacco. He looked out to his Ford. Trailer stacked with copper wiring. Copper got you paid, four dollars a pound. A sexy thing with shorts cut way up ordered something with whipped cream and the cowboy lingered for a second, then checked his watch. In fifteen minutes he'd find Marie sitting across from him with the papers and he didn't want that. He rubbed his temples, feeling where his eyebrows used to be, before all of his hair fell out and he was left looking like a boiled egg.

When he looked up, the sexy thing was in pieces against the wall, mixing with the blood and body parts of the barista. A black ball cap with the chain insignia rolled to a halt on the tiled floor. The cowboy didn't blink. Colt out, safety off. Bits of copper wiring tumbled through the destroyed wall. He fired three rounds into the spaghetti noodle swiping away from him, through the coffee shop's floor-to-ceiling windows.

He kept firing, emptying all nine rounds into the noodle.

The thing disappeared over the building, then crashed down, bits of formica tabletops clattering around his boots. He tore under the shadow of the thing, giant spiderweb eyes staring down at him, the Creator and now the Destroyer. He jumped over upturned Civics and got his door open. Bullets in the floor. Ejected the casing. He thumbed the rounds in, turned, and the noodle had him, had him in the air, bleeding from his nose, ears and eyes, and then he was falling.

Three days earlier, reclined in his chair, the cowboy had what he believed to be indigestion. He took his shirt off and ran his face under the tap. He walked down the stairs, the sun irritating his burns, and laid out by the pool. His apartment complex was dead but for a young girl floating on a pink dinosaur. He pulled out his cell phone, the screen dark for the midday sun, and shaded it with his palm. He sent a text to a few of his buddies at work, his two sons, his neighbor. He sat the phone down and dipped in the pool. His chest still burned, even underwater. He toweled off, the pool now deserted. He writhed in bed for the next three days, his chest feeling as though it were splitting apart, the only thing keeping him from the hospital his lack of insurance.

On the third day, bald, eyebrowless, with the pain gone, he ventured to the coffee shop to meet Marie. And as he spun in the blue sky, vomiting over himself and into space, he felt the burn again, quicker and harder. His chest came apart, the center becoming two parentheses, warm wet pink in the center. Thumping. He felt it in his mind then, every angle of the ground below him sharp. He kept the sacred geometry, carried the mark on his chest. This life, the time in the sheet metal plant, the time laying fencepost, meeting Marie in that neon bar while the live band played and he stumbled with his liquor, the birth of their children, that gradual aching drift that set them apart, everything. Nothing. He kept the vesica, he kept it for this moment, and when the spaghetti noodle approached him, the moist white tentacle shrunk to nothing, lost inside the hole in his chest. The flying monster panicked but no amount of pulling could keep it from the center. It disappeared into his chest, and the cowboy plummeted to earth.

BLOODSKELETON, SCOURGE OF THE CHRISTIES

by Marc Levinthal

The great sandship Wallmart groaned and rumbled, turning in a wide arc across the crimson desert. The sacred Jollyhead, skull and crossed bones, billowed in the fading sun, high above wind-filled sails drenched in orange glow as if lit from within. All around, impaled on rigging and masts, were the heads of the infidels, mute witnesses to the awesome power and light of the Most High Volant Pasta Lord.

Exxon McDonalds, known far and wide as the infamous Captain Bloodskeleton, twisted the great wheel in the direction of the setting sun. He peered across The Great Vague-Ass Waste, tracking the horizon, hoping for a sign of more christies. He'd seen smoke curl from a meager cookfire far to the south, as the first rays of the sun globe had struggled up from the green gloom over the eastern mountains. But the infidels had caught his scent, and were long gone by the time the Wallmart arrived. His men found a mound of ashes, coals still burning underneath, but no sign of which way the christies had gone.

It was as if they'd vanished into thin air.

It had been a long, hot, wasted day. No harvest for the Great Flyer. He mouthed a silent prayer for forgiveness, and another for understanding.

When would the christies stop their blasphemy and come to the One True? Only then could he cease his endless pursuit, the endless bloodshed. He was a holy pirate, true, but he took no pleasure in killing. Pillaging, now that was another story. He kind of liked that.

His thoughts turned to the blasphemy itself—he knew the christies' creed well—the better to know his enemy. He pictured it then: silvery Jesse Christie, racing across the heavens, dying on his fiery cross as he falls, a strange visitor from another planet. As he dies, he descends into his icy fortress at the south pole.

And even now the christies awaited his return, when he will transform into a fat, bearded elf in a red and white suit, who in a single night will fly his chariot all over the world, delivering magical baskets of candy, bestowing immortal, incorruptible bodies upon all who eat of it.

He shook his head, and spit onto the deck. Such a preposterous image.

There'd been no clue to the christies' whereabouts, but Bloodskeleton's instincts told him to follow the sun, head toward the great water, and so he'd swung the ship about. Something was waiting there, just over the horizon. He knew it.

One of the men suddenly cried out from the crow's nest— he'd spied a copse of palm trees in the distance. They made for it, and found a small oasis there, a hot spring and a well, and an Elvi.

He stood in a clearing under some palm trees, dancing his odd dervish peppered with strange moves, the trance-inducing karate-dancing of his order. He was barefoot, and wore a faded, tattered jumpsuit festooned with rhinestones, his skin filthy and his hair coiffed up over his head in a mud plaster.

The crew spilled out of the sandship to take up defensive positions around the oasis. Bloodskeleton jumped down the gangplank and approached the man.

The Elvi appeared untroubled. His order was revered by christie and Pastafarian alike, their namesake considered a prophet by both—even sand pirates would not dare to harm a holy one, especially one so favored by the Most High.

"Ahwellahwella hey..." chanted the Elvi as he waved his hands over his head in blessing. "Ahdonbe cruel awhella. Bigabigah hunka love will do."

Bloodskeleton focused on the odd speech. Elvi only spoke in the words of their sacred texts, and so used a kind of code to indicate what they really meant. This one was formally indicating his hope that the pirates would respect him and leave him unharmed.

"Aarrr," Bloodskeleton snarled by way of greeting, replying in the High Pirate dialect. "Ye'll be tellin' us now if you've spied any christies and where they be bound, and we'll be on our way. No harm will come to ye."

The Elvi wiggled back and forth a few times, threw a few more karate moves. "I-I-I'm caught in a trap," he spouted finally. Then he stood very still, crouched with his arms held in front of him. "I can't walk out."

Just then, all hell broke loose as an army of pigtailed little girls in frilly pastel dresses, giant machetes held over their heads, ran screaming out from behind boulders and trees, hacking expertly at the pirates' legs, severing tendons and dropping them, then deftly lopping off their heads. The Elvi started to run, but only made it a few feet. His freshly-hewn head rolled up to the toe of Bloodskeleton's dusty boot, staring up with a surprised look on its face.

"Aar, Great Belial's testicles!" Bloodskeleton cursed, un-sheathing his sword. "Blasted Vivian Girls!"

About half of the pirates, those that hadn't been slaughtered in the first moments of the sneak attack, swung axes, swords and truncheons at the horde of gen-engineered attackers. One look into the snarling face of one of them was enough to confirm what Bloodskeleton already knew: these were little girls in appearance only, battle-hardened assassins, fanatical Dargerite zealots, products of the Great Art Wars, some old enough that they might as well be immortal.

Bloodskeleton waded into the fray, swinging his sword back and forth, wheeling around, sending up streamers of blood and gore as the Vivians tried to surround him. He'd fought them many times before, and each time felt no less terror.

Then he heard a telltale rhythmic whining from somewhere behind the boulders. It was getting louder, closer. Now a lower-pitched whirring.

"Oh, great steaming turd of a winged pig!"

How could this get any worse? he wondered. *Dogs. Big dogs and little dogs, from the sound of it.*

The robots loped into the fray, motorized death-dealers, two- and four-legged machine guns with legs, spraying hot lead as they went, mowing down pirates and the occasional Vivian Girl unlucky enough to get in the way.

Bloodskeleton, having cleared away the immediate clutch of girl assassins and finding himself in a momentary lull while a new enthusiastic group sprinted toward him, reached into the side pocket of his long robe and pulled out a death egg, which he'd stashed there for just such an occasion. He pressed an indent on the side of it, saw the flashing red light and lobbed it at the nearest oncoming big dog, flinging himself on the ground just in time to feel the concussion pound him, hear the deafening boom, then the shower of meat gobbet plops and hot clanking metal. Thanking the Volant Lord he was still in one piece, he got up, ears ringing, gore-soaked, and began to run shakily in the direction of the sandship.

He got to it just ahead of a small clutch of Vivians, and pulled up the gangplank. A handful of his men had gotten there before him, and were now manning the guns to the port and starboard.

"Weigh anchor and hoist the mizzen, me hearties!" Bloodskeleton screamed. The crew, preoccupied with gunning down the Vivians who were attempting to scale the sides of the ship and blowing up the dogs who were doing their best to blast the ship to splinters, ignored the captain. Bloodskeleton bellowed in frustration and set about hoisting the anchor himself. He managed to get it almost up over the side, and then raced over to raise the sail, when a low rumbling started up and grew, rocking the length of the ship.

The Vivians dropped from the ship and scattered in all directions. One of the pirates screamed, and pointed to the northwest, to the mountain foothills.

Rocks, bushes, boulders and dirt tumbled down the side and an immense shadow curled over the top of a mountain. Then another to its right. Then another shadow, and another. Long, flowing mounds of skin began to ripple over the side and down the steep incline, growing in height as more flesh appeared over the top.

Six behemoths ploughed down the mountainside, jiggling pyramids of flesh: bodymod plastisurges, products of the excesses of the Gentech Dynasties, huge colonies of subsumed bodies, minds slaved in series, superprocessor serving one overmind.

Bloodskeleton managed to rouse himself and hoist the sail, take the wheel and steer the ship. The great vessel inched forward, gaining speed as the wind billowed in the sails and the giant wheels below grabbed the sand and gained momentum.

But all efforts were in vain—the first pyramidal monstrosity burst forward at incredible speed, overtaking the sandship and pushing its bulk in front of it. There was nothing to be done: the great ship slammed into the meat mountain, groaning and cracking as it splintered and burst apart.

Bloodskeleton lunged forward as the deck beneath him came apart, falling through the crumbling deck to what he knew to be his certain doom. He plummeted downward, then suddenly was plucked from the air, wind knocked out of his chest at the abrupt halt, as a stinking, rough tentacle-tongue wrapped around his torso and dragged him down into the fetid nether-regions of the plastisurge. Terror gripped him, and darkness descended, consciousness fading....

He woke, instantly retching, his nose assailed by the vomitous stench of the plastisurge's slimy holding pouch.

Bloodskeleton stood up shakily and looked around him. He was alone in a chamber of flesh, maybe ten feet across, judging from what little he could see in the feeble pinkish light leaking through the membranous wall. There was no telling how long he'd been unconscious. He felt motion beneath him: the slow, undulating forward motion of the great meat-mountain.

Slowly, his memories returned to him. His ship was smashed, his crew slaughtered, and he'd been sucked up into this hideous womb bound for Monster knew where...

Dejectedly, he curled himself into a ball on the wet floor of the pouch, conserving his energy, awaiting whatever horrible fate was in store for him.

He dozed uneasily, and might have even slept, but before long, he felt the floor tipping, his feet and legs being sucked down into an unseen sphincter.

Soon his entire body was being pushed through the disgusting, viscous tube, peristaltic contractions moving him along, until finally, he fell with a thud onto cracked, ancient pavement.

He lay there, recovering himself, finally sitting up, relieved to find that nothing was broken. He was bruised, sodden and smelly, but intact. Bloodskeleton stood up and looked around, gasping in surprise despite himself.

He was standing on a wide thoroughfare. Up and down the avenue were tall, wide temples, with hundreds of rows of windows, each lit with myriad candles and flares. The plastisurges had moved off down the middle of the great road, barely able to clear each side, herded away by men in red suits with matching pillbox hats who carried long sparking prods. Bloodskeleton doubted the electrical shocks could do the meat-mountains any harm, or even cause any discomfort. He thought they must merely guide them in the direction the shepherds wanted them to go.

Three of the men in the odd costumes surrounded him, brandishing their lightning sticks.

Bloodskeleton scowled at them. "Avast. Keep yer puny phalluses in yer pants, lubbers."

They growled at him, drawing closer, the lightning sticks inches from him now.

He tried to address them in the low speech. "Dudes. WTF? Chill, all right?" This only proved to make them more impatient. One of them zapped him, making him cry out, then gestured down the wide avenue.

He decided the best course of action was to move in the indicated direction. Evidently, they wanted him alive, or they would have killed him by now. He still had his sword, concealed between his outer robe and pantaloons. But if he struck out now, he might only succeed in taking a couple of them with him to his doom. It made the most sense to play along until he could find a means of escape.

He walked along in front of his captors, gazing around at the tall buildings, the elaborate dry fountains (which must have once defied the desert with copious sprays of perfumed waters), the towering statues of the pagan celebrigods: The Elvis, Mother Marilyn, the Four Horsemen of the Liver-Pool. Now he knew where he'd been taken by the plastisurge. He was in the very heart of the Great Desert Sixty-Six, in the center of the Lost Vague-Ass.

He would find no allies here. No one to save him. This was the land of the Suits, servants of the MJ, the Pop King, Chairman of the Bored.

As if on queue, a long chariot of black, shiny metal, a relic from the Golden Days, passed him, pulled by several of the red-capped men. Through the open windows, Bloodskeleton saw several of the Suits lounging inside. At some unseen signal, the chariot—he thought the proper name was "leemo"—came to a stop.

A door was opened by a redcap, and out of it stepped one of the noblemen of this place. He wore the ancient traditional costume: a coat and matching pants of fine, thin, almost irridescent fabric, and a peculiar thin strip of dark fabric tied around the neck, under a collared shirt. He wore dark eyeglasses that curved over the bridge of his nose and swept behind his ears.

The man stepped up to Bloodskeleton, took a sniff and waved a hand in front of him. "Whoa," he said, "Whoa. Fuggetaboudit." He smiled. "Hey, Tony," he called to someone inside the carriage, "we got a fuckin' pirate out heah." He turned to the nearest redcap. "Take him over to the Palace," he said. "The Chairman will smile upon us today." He bowed his head and held his hands out in front of him. "May Old Blue Eyes and His Pack of Rats be praised."

The Suit climbed back into the leemo and it departed.

Bloodskeleton was led further down the broad avenue, then prodded through the door of one of the temples, into a broad room filled with the sounds of ringing bells. Hundreds of acolytes manned square chiming machines, creating the cacaphony by pulling long handles on the sides of them. Hundred of candles lit the cavernous chamber, driving the desert heat to ennervating extremes, the space filled with the fetid exhalations and rancid body odors of the pitiful monks.

One of the redcaps zapped him again and shoved him toward a door marked "Exit," a word from the old speech. He knew it meant "a way out," but a way out to where? Were they taking him to this Chairman, hoping to gain information? He knew the Suits were no lovers of the christies, so maybe he could strike some kind of bargain, maybe even convince them to join forces with him, somehow come to an arrangement that would benefit all.

They went out the door, into a white hallway, and up a staircase that ascended for several floors. Finally they emerged into blue-bright daylight, on a wide expanse of rooftop. There, throngs of disheveled, long-haired men and women, some in robes and furs, some naked and painted, cavorted to the beats and ululations of strange music, a din of thrashed and scraped metal, and shrill horns.

Many of them carried flowers or small shrubs in pots, with pale green filaments trailing away from plants' stems to fleshy mounds behind their ears. Near another stairway a little way off, Suits took tribute of one kind or another from the disheveled ones, letting them onto the roof one at a time, releasing them from a queue that led back down the stairwell.

Toward the back of the large space, in a huge metal enclosure, an immense wooden structure towered: the effigy of a man. At the base of it, more wood was piled. Bloodskeleton looked back at one of the redcaps, who grinned wickedly at his dawning realization. It was an elaborate pyre, and he was to be the sacrifice.

There would be no parlay. No one to save him, no one to bargain with. He would merely be part of the evening's entertainment for this flock of disheveled wildmen.

He wished in vain for one more of the death eggs—but he'd only carried the one. He still had his sword; they'd never searched him, the stupid bastards. Maybe he could still take down three or four of these sissies before he himself was struck down, and at least deny them the pleasure of watching him burn.

They turned him, marching him through the gyrating throng. Many of them seemed not to notice him, especially the ones holding the plants; they seemed not to notice much of anything. Bloodskeleton had heard of McKennas, but had never actually seen one. They were yet another blasphemous cult, worshippers of the Plant Intelligence, who claimed direct contact with the vast wisdom of the earth. He looked at one, blissed out and oblivious, and wondered if it could be true. If there was wisdom in this one, it was well concealed.

Anyway, it didn't matter. He was going to die now, one way or another. So if he could choose his doom, he would. He looked up at the effigy of the man that would burn when the sun went down.

It would have to be now.

Now.

As his hand swept down for his sword, he heard surprised cries and saw outstretched arms pointing into the sky. There was a buzzing, a whirring noise growing louder, then almost deafening, and pinpoints all over the sky resolved themselves as they grew larger, revealing themselves to be figures with autogyros strapped to their backs, descending like locusts from the west, from exactly the angle and direction of the sun, so as to better blind the defenders.

Then the pop-pop, the whistle and dull thud of bullets hitting flesh. All around him, the redcaps and the wild men fell. He threw his arms over his head in a futile effort to defend himself, running for the cover of the giant man effigy. Hidden in the shadow of the wicker behemoth, Bloodskeleton shaded his eyes and looked up. Now the attack force blackened the sky from north to south like a plague of locusts. Quickly, the great horde descended, fanning out across the streets and rooftops.

Bloodskeleton praised his Monster as he realized who exactly these attackers were: priest warriors of the Most High, long white dreadlocks flaring around their heads, stylized to mimic the riots of holy noodles, dark-brown meatball pants-armour obscuring their bodies, cultivated eyestalks curling and undulating above their heads, scimitars raised and voices lustily screaming out the holy "R'aaaamennnnnn!"

The warriors made quick work of the rooftop revelers, either finishing off those that remained standing, or herding and binding them together into groups.

Bloodskeleton drew his sword and waited while three of the Lord's Warriors sprinted toward him, guns at the ready. But when they drew near, they lowered their weapons and bowed to him.

The nearest warrior addressed him. "We have been following you for days, Bloodskeleton," he said. "The Lord has marked you as most worthy, most worthy indeed. You have wiped out the unbelievers far and wide, left a trail of infidel's blood in great swaths across the desert. And for this, you shall be this day with the One True God in Paradise. We shall load the belly of this effigy with the Heathen, but you shall sit in the place of honor in its head, the worthy sacrifice unto the Volant Pasta Beast. Rejoice, Bloodskeleton. Rejoice!"

As the flames licked at his boots, Captain Exxon McDonalds, known far and wide as Bloodskeleton the Pirate, steeled himself against the momentary pain, knowing that he was a chosen one, that soon he would be frolicking in the endless, all-nourishing volcano of beer, cavorting with the Prophet Henderson in the Manufactory of Holy Houris. He would live there, in the prescence of the One True Monster, in bliss, forever and ever.

Bloodskeleton had been saved. The Lord was all powerful, all good, a just Lord.

In those last moments, he reflected upon the multitudes of infidels he had dispatched. They numbered in the thousands. And they had deserved their fate—thou shalt have no other monsters before me, sayeth the lord. When would the infidels learn to praise the one true God? Had the ceaseless slaughter taught them nothing?

It might take centuries, he decided, but one day, the Pirate's Creed would envelope the world entirely, and all would know the glory and the truth of the one true God, the one true Flying Spaghetti Monster.

He smiled, at peace, as the flames took him.

DOWN AND OUT IN MYTHOS CITY

by Adam Bolivar

The Flying Spaghetti Monster—Frank to his friends—sat slumped in a piss-stinking back alley behind an Italian restaurant. He took a swig from a two-dollar bottle of vodka, clutched precariously in a limp noodly hand. Like so many aspiring deities before him, Frank had come to Mythos City for a shot at godhood, only to have his hopes crushed underfoot like an empty beer can. He thought back to the Inquiry, and took a long pull from his bottle. The liquor stung his twelfth-of-an-inch-wide throat and combined with the pureed tomato inside his stomach to form a delicious vodka sauce.

The Octagon had tasteful teak-paneled walls and gothic stained glass windows, which gave it the hushed grandeur of a cathedral. On each of the eight sides of the chamber was a high-backed oaken throne nicely padded with velvet cushions. The petitioner sat in the center of the Octagon in a squeaky swivel chair.

Frank had applied for the Inquiry thirty-seven times, and had received thirty-seven xeroxed form letters politely rejecting him. Finally, his thirty-eighth application was accepted, as likely as not to stop him from sending in more applications. He didn't care. Godhood was the most prestigious club on earth. The fact that Frank, the Flying Spaghetti Monster from Piscataway, New Jersey had a shot to make his case before eight bona fide gods was the dream of a lifetime.

As the gods started making their way into the Octagon, it was all Frank could do to keep from wetting himself out of excitement. First came Thor, tossing back his streaming locks of heavily moussed blonde hair. His pink, Louis Vuitton shirt was unbuttoned almost down to his belly button, revealing a chest of ripping, six-pack abs.

The Norse god of lightning sat down in the throne directly in front of Frank, and gave the floppy mass of spaghetti noodles a glare that could melt lead. Thor's knuckles whitened as he gripped the handle of his enchanted hammer Mjöllnir. He didn't like giving up a day of golfing on the fields of Asgard to deal with this bureaucratic bullshit. Frank rocked nervously in his chair. Things were not off to a good start.

The next god to enter was Athena, the representative from the Greek pantheon. Flinging aside a pair of Ray Ban sunglasses, she flopped into the throne on Thor's right. She shared her fellow deity's contemptuous expression.

"Can you believe this shit?" she asked him. "And on a Sunday! I was on my way to Samos to spend the day at the beach."

"Tell me about it," Thor replied, shooting Frank another evil look. "I guess it's in our contract or something that we have to do this pro bono crap."

"Whatever. As soon as I'm out of here, I'm calling my agent."

Next was an old man with wild white hair and a long white beard. He looked a little like Santa Claus, except that he was wearing a blue pinstriped Brooks Brothers suit. Checking his Rolex impatiently, he hiked up his expensive trousers so they wouldn't wrinkle, and settled himself into the throne next to Athena. Being the sole deity of three of the world's major religions had a lot of perks, but it also meant that he had to come to every one these damn Inquiries. YHVH couldn't rotate the duty with other members of a pantheon. Well, there was J.C., but good luck getting *him* to do a day's work.

One by one, the rest of the gods filed in. Elephant-headed Ganesha took a seat, never once looking up from his Blackberry. A beer-bellied Buddha wearing an Adidas track suit jogged in, huffing and puffing. Joseph Smith strode in gracefully and took his seat. He wore a neat black suit, white shirt and a black tie. He took an iPhone from his suit pocket and set it to silent.

The next god to enter was Cthulhu, who came shuffling in wearing fuzzy bunny slippers and a tent-sized Calvin Klein bathrobe wrapped around his squamous green torso. Membranous wings poked out of two tailored slits in the back of the robe. Cthulhu sank into his throne gelatinously and yawned. He didn't appreciate being woken up before the stars were right.

Finally, Charlie Sheen stumbled in wearing a "WINNING" T-shirt and a backwards-facing baseball cap. He gave the Buddha a high five and sat down in the last remaining throne. His eyes were bloodshot and he looked as if he could pass out at any moment.

Thor cleared his throat. "Okay, let's get this over with. As this week's Chairperson, I call the thirty-eight thousand nine hundred and fifty-fifth Assembly of United Deities to order." He used his hammer as a gavel and struck the block of wood specially installed in the armrest of his throne. A booming crescendo of thunder filled the Octagon. Thor loved that. He grinned like a little boy on Christmas morning. Athena rolled her eyes.

"We are gathered to hear the plea of the party known as the, ahem, Flying Spaghetti Monster, who petitions to join our august company under Article 52 of the Charter of Confederated Pantheons…"

"Yes, yes," YHVH interrupted in a deep gravelly voice that sounded suspiciously like a movie trailer narrator. "We all know what the charter says. Can we get on with it? This whole thing is a sham anyway. There is only one true God."

"Stick a sock in it, Joe," Ganesha said in a lilting Indian accent. "Your one true God schtick is getting old."

"I'm a warlock!" Charlie Sheen shouted, apropos of nothing. He had fallen asleep in his chair and been woken up by his cigarette smoldering down to the filter and burning his fingers. "Fastball! I'm a warlock with tiger's blood. Winning!"

"For fuck's sake," Athena said, rubbing her temples and wishing she had a bottle of vicodin handy. "Do we really have to put up with this asshole?"

Just then, two black-robed monks entered the chamber. Their hoods were raised to conceal their faces. Each monk grabbed hold of one of Charlie Sheen's arms and began dragging him from the Octagon.

"Finally," Athena said. "Godhood revoked. Winning!"

"Fuck you, bitch!" Charlie Sheen yelled.

Athena gave him the middle finger and smiled. She was in a much better mood now.

A few seconds later, Elvis Presley stepped through the door and sat down in the empty throne. He was a late-period Elvis, and wore a hideous white jumpsuit decorated with rhinestones. He pointed his index finger at Frank and winked. "Thank you very much," he said.

"Anyhoo," Thor said. "If we can proceed now. I'd like to get back to my weekend while there are a few hours of daylight left."

"Hear, hear," Athena seconded.

"We should throw this case out right now," YHVH said. "The petition is ludicrous. Nobody seriously believes in the

Flying Spaghetti Monster. He's a joke concocted by atheists to make fun of the whole idea of gods."

Atheists were a pet peeve of YHVH's. As were homosexuals. And people who ate pork. And menstruating women. And kittens. Every time YHVH saw a kitten, he just wanted to kick its fucking head like a football.

"To be fair," Ganesha chimed in. "So was Cthulhu. But enough people started believing in him that he became a real god."

"Ph'nglui mglw'nafh Cthulhu R'lyeh wgah'nagl fhtagn," Cthulhu agreed.

"Riiight," YHVH said. "But my point is, there's still nobody who actually believes in the Flying Spaghetti Monster. He has no churches, no temples, no holidays, nothing. The frickin' Tooth Fairy has a better claim to being a god. Not that there are any gods but me..."

"That's enough of that," Thor said. "You can save that bullshit for your worshippers. Let's keep things civil in here."

"Fine, fine." YHVH smiled smarmily, holding up his hand and examining his perfectly manicured fingernails. "Have it your way. Anyway, you know what my vote will be."

Thor turned to Frank. "Would the petitioner like to say anything before we cast the vote?"

Frank's legs went wobbly like two strands of spaghetti. Oh wait—they *were* two strands of spaghetti. He had rehearsed so many arguments in his hotel room the night before. But now, on his big day in the Octagon, he was drawing a blank.

"Er... um..." Frank said. "Well... I do have a holiday. It's International Talk Like a Pirate Day. Arrr, matey. Pieces of eight. Polly want a cracker?"

You could have heard a pin drop.

"Okaaay," Thor said, looking at Frank like he had two enormous meatballs in place of a head, which in fact he did. "On the matter of conferring the status of godhood upon the

Flying Spaghetti Monster, how does the Assembly of United Deities vote?"

Athena looked up from filing her nails. "Oh, is this still going on?" She gave Frank an appraising look and chuckled. "Sorry, dear. Nay."

"NAY!" YHVH boomed in his best Voice-of-God voice.

Ganesha shrugged. "Nay."

"The thousand petals of the lotus blossom open," the Buddha said. "And the jewel within is no jewel. Sorry. I mean, nay."

"Aye," said Joseph Smith.

"N'gaaah!" roared Cthulhu, his face-tentacles writhing like a pit of vipers.

"I'll have a fried peanut butter and banana sandwich," said Elvis. "Thank you very much."

"Nay," said Thor. "So that's one aye, six nays, and one fried peanut and banana sandwich. The nays have it. No godhood."

Thor slammed his hammer down, punctuating the judgment with a dramatic peal of thunder. The gods turned their backs on Frank and began filing out of the Octagon.

"Hey baby," Thor said to Athena. "Do you like my hammer?"

"Sorry, hon. The handle is a little shorter than I'm used to."

And then they were gone. Frank was alone. Alone in the Octagon, just as he lived alone in a tiny apartment in Piscataway. Just as he sat alone in a back alley, with only a bottle of cheap vodka for company. He had been so stupid to quit his job at Kinko's and fly to Mythos City with his stupid dream of becoming a god. Stupid, stupid, stupid! And now he'd just spent his last two stupid dollars on a bottle of stupid vodka and the stupid bottle was empty. Frank hurled the bottle at the brick wall across from him. But his floppy wrist was too weak to throw it with any force, and it fell short, clinking on the ground without breaking.

"Hey, man, do you have a lighter?"

Frank looked up to see a familiar-looking man standing over him. The man had long scraggly hair and a beard, and wore a tie-dyed T-shirt and blue jeans so worn out they barely covered his legs anymore. A total hippie, in other words. And to complete the image, he held a glass pipe in his hand. It was packed with fragrant emerald-green nugs.

"No, I'm afraid not," Frank replied. He'd even failed at that. He felt like bursting into tears.

"It's all good," said the hippie. Jesus Christ, Frank suddenly realized. It was Jesus Christ! Jesus handed Frank the pipe and snapped his fingers. A tiny yellow flame blossomed miraculously from his thumb. Jesus winked. "Four-twenty, man."

Frank had quit smoking pot months ago in case he was drug-tested for the Inquiry. But what did it matter now? He put the pipe between his lips and Jesus obligingly lowered his flaming thumb to the bowl. Frank sucked hard and started coughing like a motherfucker. Oh yeah, that was some good shit. Jesus took a hit too, and then passed the pipe back to Frank. They got a couple more hits each before the bowl was cashed. Then they leaned back against the wall and enjoyed the moment.

Frank had been so focused on preparing for the Inquiry, he had failed to notice how beautiful Mythos City was. Majestic, snow-peaked Mount Olympus loomed overhead. The gold towers of Valhalla glinted in the light of the setting sun. Bifrost, the rainbow bridge cascaded from Valhalla's gate like a Technicolor river. Even the faceted crystal dome that housed the Octagon, the source of so much anxiety for him, looked beautiful now, like a giant glittering diamond.

"You're the new god on the block, right?" Jesus asked.

"I wanted to be a god," Frank said. "But they voted against me."

"Fuck 'em. Who cares what those dickheads think? If you

want to be a god, then be a god. No one's stopping you."

"Wow, I never thought of it that way before." Frank's mind was whirling like a dervish. Dude, it all made so much sense now.

"Being a god's not all it's cracked up to be, anyway. My dad wanted me to be a god. Make it into a family business. God and Son, Inc. But what did I get out of it? Forty lashes and nailed to a fucking cross! It was bullshit, man. I told my dad to shove it and went on Dead Tour. Best decision of my life. Jerry Garcia—now there's a god for you."

Frank had to pee. There was a back door to the restaurant in the alley. He thought he'd duck inside and see if he could find a bathroom. As he got up to leave, Jesus grabbed his wrist and pulled him close.

"A word of advice, kid. If you really want to be a god, you need a story. Pluck out your eye. Make a sacrifice. Something. It doesn't have to be huge. Just plant a seed, you dig?"

Frank had no idea what Jesus was talking about, but it sounded deep. He walked through the door into a kitchen. On the stovetop, a large pot of water bubbled fiercely. A sacrifice, huh?

The Flying Spaghetti Monster died for your sins. Eat this pasta, for it is my body.

For the first time in his life, Frank took a leap of faith. And half an hour later, a tourist from Wichita had the best spaghetti dinner of his life.

COVEN OF THE CRAWLING PIZZA BEAST

by Edmund Colell

Sal feels the guillotine clave before the tomato sauce spills out of his neck. The sauce carries his thoughts: *They really weren't joking. I was just sacrificed by a pizza cult.* The rest of his being spills together as black-capped people roll up his legs, and then the rest of his body, until all tomato sauce is squeezed away from his skin and bones.

The pizza dough beneath his sauce begins to rise. One of the cap-wearing figures says, "Delicious beast, hungry beast, your meat lover pleases the cosmic belly! Now rise, rise as the cooked air cooks you!"

Sal smells alcohol as the dough bubbles beneath him. *Damn, all of the senses and none of the body... I think I'm being too fascinated by this.*

One alcohol bubble grows lips, sucking in Sal's sauce as the lips open. Sal feels a tingle, though he cannot move as the lips suck him up. However, the bubble soon stops sucking and says, "Yarrgh! Few men have zest in their sauce quite like a pirate!"

Pirate? A pizza bubble is talking to me about pirates?

"Aye, Laddie. And no, this whole thing is not a dream. This is the reality of yer being the last pirate on Earth. At least, yeh *were* the last pirate on Earth."

Sal reviews his life: a bullied childhood, a passing adolescence, and an ongoing office internship supported by pizza delivery. In that reflection, he thinks to slap himself for following his manager to the meet-up for the Coven of the Crawling Pizza Beast. His manager, Dan, had promised "many people eagerly awaiting your sauce. Your delicious, delicious sauce." *A boring life punctuated at the end by a semen joke. How does that make me a pirate?*

"No jokes or semen here, boy. The mark of a true-blooded pirate is a body full of tomato sauce. I myself used to be the sauciest pirate of the seven seas and six food groups. They called me only by the name of Bigoli Beard. But then, they of the Coven of the Crawling Pizza Beast corrupted me. They convinced me to steal music from an accordion player—stolen music be the headiest drug any pirate has ever known—and then they dried me sauce from me bones and ground me into the dough of the Crawling Pizza Beast."

Why in the hell would they do that?

"Laddie, wouldn't yeh murder yer competitors if it made yer product better and yeh could get away with it?"

Not really.

"Neither would I, but they of the Coven have done it forever! Yer books tried to make the pirate battles look like squabbles for wealth and slaves when in fact the great battles of spaghetti and pizza were being waged."

So were we killing people for spaghetti?

"Killing only in defense, my boy. Ours is the sauce, ours is the power. In time, yer sauce will learn the power to summon the Second Serving of the Flying Spaghetti Monster from the belly of the Beast and end the scourge of global warming which yer death begat. In the name of the pirates, and the pasta, and the sacred sauce, R'amen."

As the sun continues to bake the air, the Crawling Pizza Beast rises and growls. Dan revs up a chainsaw and says, "Our Beast is hungry! It desires meat!"

Sal soon feels twitching masses of cut-up bodies spilling into his sauce. Their body fat melts, forming splotches like cheese over him. Bigoli Beard says, "Follow me down, through the yeast-born alcohol," and vanishes. Sal feels for the nearest bubble and spills his consciousness into a single dollop of sauce. He drops in, landing in an alcohol pit. Bones form out of the dough, followed by a naval hat topping the skull and strands of spaghetti dangling off the chin like a beard. The dough-skeleton plops in and says, "Yeh mind makin' some room?"

"How do I do that? I'm a liquid."

"If yeh can make yerself solid, yeh can do everything else. The Crawling Pizza Beast will win if yeh don't."

Sal pulls his concentration toward a humanoid shape. Fingers and toes soon emerge, then a head. Just as Sal's mental stamina starts to tire, Bigoli Beard says through a flapping jaw, "Picture this bread booze as the best beer to ever fondle yer tongue."

Sal imagines those exact words and tastes his memories. Strong, dark, bitter, and full of froth. The alcohol thickens into foam as it takes on various flavors from Sal's fantasies. The beer rises until he is standing almost shoulder-deep in the thick liquid.

"Errr..." Bigoli Beard mutters with foam in one hand, "Didn't know yeh liked this kind o' beer. Could'a been better if..." he shakes his head. "Nevermind. Beer is beer in a pirate's mind. Now yeh understand the sauce's power."

"It turns us into Christ figures who can create beer out of nothing?"

"Only within this Pizza Beast. Made it sick with me bones.

The fools who killed yeh forgot I was here."

Sal lathers some of the foam and rubs it over his face. "Gotta say the being-a-dead-pirate thing is pretty sweet so far. I never thought I'd make a beer bath just by thinking about it."

Bigoli Beard slams his fist through the foam and shouts, "Bite yer dreamy tongue! I want to see some fuckin' action outta yeh!"

"Dude, if I knew what a sauce-pirate was supposed to do, I'd do it."

Bigoli Beard sighs. His bones dissolve back into the walls. "The last pirate wants everything handed to him."

Sal splashes the wall and shouts, "Do you want me to do this right or not? Seriously, if I'm doing badly as the last pirate, I don't know how to fix that."

Outside, Dan marches alongside the Crawling Pizza Beast. He twirls his ceremonial global-warming-proof chainsaw, whistling as people run and collapse in the heat. He hacks at the weakened victims and tosses their severed parts atop the Pizza Beast's bubbling layer of cheese-like fat.

Soon Dan shuts off his chainsaw and produces a megaphone. "The cosmos has made its order!" he preaches. "We are not worthy of tips, but their bill is great! Our pizza for their blessings, in forty hours or less!"

Car-deprived cops rush into the streets, bullets bursting from their overheated guns. Left only with their batons against Dan's chainsaw, they scatter with dry screams.

In his pit of beer, Sal imagines an eye patch forming over his faceless sauce-head. The eye patch is half-formed, a tomato tumor strapped across his face. "Arrgh," he says, feeling a shade of minimal effort weaken his voice. "Keelhauled booty off the port bow. Wenches and ale flowing out my booty." The eye patch solidifies, though it is still made of tomato product.

A great glob of fat splashes into the pit with him. He hears a faint sucking as the fat soaks up some beer. "Oh hell no," he growls as he picks it up and tries to launch it back to the surface. His wrists pop off without pain as the fat glob ascends a short height and plummets back into the beer. The fat soaks up more beer, and Sal's dismembered hands mold the fat into a bulbous humanoid. Head, legs, arms, breasts, and a chubby gut. His hands spread themselves into a bra and pair of panties. Soon the fat fondles its new breasts and giggles, "Your touch tickled me back to life!"

A penis-shaped pillar of sauce rises up to the canopy of the pit. The fatty girl wraps a leg around the solid sauce pole and spins around it. Her yellow tongue licks the pole and her hands stroke it. A Jolly Roger hat inflates on top of Sal's head.

"So..." Sal says, "I kinda get the deal with Bigoli Beard, but what are you supposed to be?"

The fatty girl steadies herself on her feet and asks, "What do you mean? Do I need a reason for being here? Would you like me better dead?"

"Lady, I would never know you from the other fat blobs above us. Don't get me wrong, I love you wearing my hands and dancing on a phallic extension of myself. All I want to know is why you went from a blob of fat to a hot chunk of woman, seeing as we're both dead and not human anymore."

"Must be something in the tickly sauce, Babe. And if I call you Babe, call me Mandie."

I'm not even gonna try to not roll with it. I make beer and strippers? Best afterlife ever. Bigoli Beard is just a crusty asshole who can't appreciate a little fun. And if I can't have any fun when I'm dead, then let this Pizza

Beast have its way. Maybe global warming and pizza is how the world needs to end.

An arrow zips by Dan's head. He turns to see a man wearing boxers and a fixed grin. A compound bow rests in his hands. "I always knew this would come in handy!" the man laughs. "They always said I should get a gun, those dumbass trigger-molesters." He knocks another arrow and takes aim. His second arrow spears into the Pizza Beast.

Dan bites his lip and revs his chainsaw. Other black-caps rush in with machetes.

The man launches one more arrow, then brandishes his bow as a club. A few jaws are smashed and a few wounds are split open, but he is soon sliced and stabbed in the arms, armpits, and thighs. Tears, sweat, and drool run down his face as Dan approaches and carves healthy chunks out of him.

"No one else had your plan," Dan says. "I hope you died thinking you were a genius."

Underwear removed, all bodily chunks nestle in the arms of Dan and the others, carried all the way up to their resting place among the Pizza Beast's toppings. Then, sobering his chainsaw rush, Dan yanks the arrow from the dough and a stream of beer flows from its wound. The first trickle of sweat drips down his fan-cooled brow. "A pirate does not know his place," he says. He scrounges in his pockets for his MP3 player and places the ear buds around the wound. But as he presses the ON button, he finds that the device no longer works. *Damn*, he thinks, *global warming not only cooks the Pizza Beast, but also cooks the electronics feeding the stolen music that I need to settle an unruly pirate.* He strokes the dough and says, "You won't be sick for too long. With some more meat and fat, you'll feel much better and tastier."

Sal feels the beer starting to thin, and Mandie's form loses its structure. The bra and panties of sauce drop from her body, in addition to the parts they were protecting. Where she was originally giving Sal a lap dance, she now falls on top of him and clings.

"Build me back up!" she shouts. "You said you could keep me alive if I kept dancing!"

"But it should be working! I felt my inner pirate! Whether it was that or post-mortem horniness, you made me feel it!"

Strands of clumpy spaghetti descend from the ceiling, carried by Bigoli Beard's skull. "Aye, that she did. But while yeh stayed here and fucked around, I kept within the walls and held the Pizza Beast's power back. The more meat it gathers, the stronger it gets. It's overpowering the sauce.

"And lookin' at yeh, I'm tired o' waitin' for yeh to get off yer arse. I'll take the rest o' yer sauce, and birth myself anew as the Flying Spaghetti Monster." With that, sauce pours down from the ceiling and into Bigoli Beard's mouth. The spaghetti on his chin lengthens and thickens as sauce drips down each strand.

Mandie attaches her disintegrating limbs to the spaghetti and regains her shape. Entire low-cut clothing articles of sauce form over her swelling body. Sal feels his pole starting to deflate as he watches her tangle herself in the beard of spaghetti.

"Flying Spaghetti Monster?" Sal asks. "How are you going to become something like that?"

"By taking action and kicking arse."

"But you told me we could only summon it."

"I'll work out the details later. Fer now, get in me mouth." Bigoli Beard's jaw drops into the beer, dunking Mandie in with it. As the mouth full of sauce plunges into the beer, the beer thickens once more. Sal tastes it, and though he finds that it tastes different, the flavor rubs him unlike any he has ever tasted. A hook replaces one hand, and a peg replaces one leg.

With that hook, he pulls Mandie back above the beer. She now has a face, and skull print decorates her garments. "Follow me in," she says, stepping behind the teeth, "unless you want to be alone in here."

Sal regards the sauce within Bigoli Beard's mouth. "So you admit that you're powerless without me," he says.

"Just yer pirate essence. I would gladly digest the whiny bitch out of yeh."

With that, Sal bubbles and charges inside, splashing into the rest of his sauce. Soon, he is rushing out of Bigoli Beard's eye sockets and nostrils. With a mighty bellow filling the rest of the chamber with alcohol, he shouts "If anyone has whined today, it's you!" Multiple hooks and cutlasses emerge from the sauce and carve Bigoli Beard out of the walls, plunging him deep into the brew.

"I don't know what yer gettin' at," Bigoli Beard says. "Yeh know I can't drown."

"No, but we can get ourselves shit-faced."

Bigoli Beard's body thins out into multiple strands of spaghetti. Mandie divides into many meatballs covered in breasts with skull nipples. And as they all feed on the beer, their spaghetti body grows. Eventually, Sal watches his vision ascend on two eye stalks made of sauce.

The Pizza Beast groans a wet groan. Strands of spaghetti start to make veins along its body, pulsing just under the crust. Dan stops decapitating a crippled puppy to turn and see a strand of spaghetti emerging from the wound where beer was spilling out earlier. With his chainsaw, he lops the strand of spaghetti off and starts carving around the outer crust to get rid of the spaghetti veins. His breathing dries as he thinks of the entity who had called in their order for the Crawling Pizza Beast. His thoughts run him pale: *If we give them a sick pizza, then all is lost! But how in the hell could an employee of mine with no real pirate spirit in him do this?* As he watches more spaghetti form out of the cut crust, he crawls on top of the Pizza Beast's body. *Fuck that, I'm stopping this at the source.*

He stands in the middle of the putrid pile of human remains and stabs his chainsaw into the middle, where a great swell pulses within. "I'm aborting this pirate child right here, right now!" he screams, as meat, sauce, and spaghetti gush over his body.

One of Sal's eye stalks is severed. Rotating blades cut deep into Bigoli Beard's spaghetti and Mandie's meatballs. Sal ducks the spaghetti back down into the depths, trying to grow more saucy eye stalks and see where the danger is coming from. It is not long before a great hole is cut into the canopy and Sal sees Dan peering down through the opened womb of beer.

Dan pulls out his cell phone, and through Sal's heightened sense of hearing, he hears Dan calling someone named "Earl." At least, that's what it sounded like. "We might need to make a new one," Dan tells the other person. "This pizza got sick with a spaghetti creature. Yeah, sorry, must've been the pirate ingredients. It can be fixed. Thank you for your patience."

With that, the chainsaw starts back up and cuts along the ceiling, until Dan jumps off, slices down the side of the crust, and turns the chainsaw back off. The protective beer drains away from Sal and the others, and the walls begin to pound as the Pizza Beast cries. He retracts all of the strands which lined the walls, and listens for Dan and the chainsaw. It is not long before Dan looks inside.

Dan's face hardens into a tough knot at the center. As he awakens his chainsaw once more, he shouts, "For fuck's sake, Sal! Did you have to usher in the Second Serving of the Flying Spaghetti Monster, just as I was about to grant Earth the favor of a being that only wanted pizza?"

Sal lurches forward with noodly appendages raised, and the combined voices of him and Bigoli Beard howl from the spaghetti body: "WE SPOIL YER PIZZA TO BEER-SOAKED SHIT IN THE NAME OF THE PIRATES, AND THE PASTA, AND THE SACRED SAUCE! R'AMEN!" Some appendages are sliced away, while others clog up the blades and trickle sauce down to the motor.

An angelic choir rendition of "oontz-oontz" club techno softens the air. The chainsaw, covered in sauce, melts away to a lollipop with "Arrgh!" stamped on the red center. Dan drops the pirate candy and backs away, limbs shrinking away from the reach of Sal's noodles. To his chagrin, his movements synchronize with the Flying Spaghetti Monster's song of "oontz-oontz, oontz-oontz."

Breaking him out of his entranced dance, his cell phone rings again. With each chime of the "knock-knock" ringtone, a fat man with gravelly hair and pudding-like skin phases further into existence. The creature opens the mouths in its hands and says, "Just wanted to check up on the pizza. I hope you all can fix what happened to...*that* mess over there."

Sal's thoughts freeze, while Bigoli Beard thinks *So that's what it comes down to. Our great enemy was but a meal fer something more powerful.* Cool air radiates from the Flying Spaghetti Monster's body. Within minutes, the hellish heat withers to a summer breeze.

Dan struggles to wet his throat. "Well, uh…we don't necessarily need global warming to cook another Crawling Pizza Beast. And there are enough heat-exhausted corpses around…"

"And the sauce of the last pirate? The ingredient you need to animate the Crawling Pizza Beast to begin with? Without whose death, there won't be enough global warming to keep the Pizza Beast hot enough for me?"

Dan blinks the first tears from his eyes and forces a smile. "Look, Urrhl, I run a pizza joint. You'd be surprised by how good our pizza can be."

"That's not what I fucking paid for! An ancient advance payment of hospitable atmosphere and intelligent life, then the answers to the meaning of your existence when I get my pizza."

Sal feels a simultaneous surge between himself, Bigoli Beard, and Mandie. An alien memory awakens and yawns through the Flying Spaghetti Monster's mouth, spoken by Sal and voiced by Mandie. "Stop trying to con the people of Earth, Urrhl. You and I both know about your drunken night together, we know how you stimulated my noodly append-ages and one thing led to another."

Urrhl's skin blushes and thickens to stickiness. "My noodly love, all I wanted was some pizza. And besides, with the right booze, we can create life on a new planet. Who gives a damn about Earth?"

"I'll teach you my love of this planet, and we will return the glory of pirates to this world."

Urrhl and the Flying Spaghetti Monster embrace, noodles and thick pudding running over each other. Sal, Bigoli Beard, and Mandie share in their pleasure and hold each other in their own spirit-tangled embrace.

As the remaining members of the Coven of the Crawling Pizza Beast disperse, throwing the hats down from their disillusioned heads, Dan digs a hand into the Crawling Pizza Beast. "Well," he says before eating, "at least one person ought to enjoy my hard work." Within seconds of ingestion, an eye patch of skin folds over his right eye. "Arrgh," he groans.

MAN AND HIS MAKER

by Bradley Sands

The Flying Spaghetti Monster flies into a bar. He is very tired from creating the Earth. All he wants is a drink to help him relax. Unfortunately, the Flying Spaghetti Monster did not create a bartender to operate the bar. Fortunately, he built the bar underneath a beer volcano. He sits on a bar stool, points a giant twisty straw into the air, and sips a quantity of beer that surpasses a single drink. It surpasses all the beer that people have drunk throughout the entirety of history. But this is not a difficult feat considering only a small quantity of history has passed since the Flying Spaghetti Monster finished creating the Earth ten minutes ago. Nevertheless, he has still drunk an excessive amount of beer. By the time the Flying Spaghetti Monster finishes drinking an excessive amount of beer, he is so drunk that he creates Earth's second bar stool so Earth's first bar stool will feel less lonely and perhaps have someone to get romantic with. But the Flying Spaghetti Monster is too drunk to remember to give the Earth's first two bar stools the ability to feel loneliness and romance. The inactivity of the two bar stools frustrates him. He totally flips out and creates someone with the ability to feel loneliness and romance. A midget who the Flying Spaghetti Monster has named Man sits down on the Earth's second bar stool. Although he has the ability to feel loneliness and romance, he does not feel any of these emotions at the present time. It is impossible for a midget to experience loneliness while he is sitting next to a Flying Spaghetti Monster. It is impossible for a midget to experience romance when there is no one around to feel romantic about. The Flying Spaghetti Monster is disappointed by his creation's lack of emotions. The midget named Man is indifferent to his lack of emotions considering he is unaware of the potential for their existence. The Flying Spaghetti Monster thinks the midget named Man might feel sad about feeling empty inside, so he passes him his giant twisty straw. The midget named Man looks at the Flying Spaghetti Monster, confused, for he does not know what to do with the giant twisty straw. The Flying Spaghetti Monster takes the giant twisty straw back from the midget named Man, puts it underneath the beer volcano, and shows his creation how to sip beer. He passes the straw back to the midget, who sips a quantity of beer that surpasses a single drink but does not surpass the quantity of beer that the Flying Spaghetti Monster drank previous to creating the midget and Earth's second stool. The midget named Man becomes extremely inebriated and makes the Flying Spaghetti Monster laugh with his drunken antics. Thus not only is the midget named Man the Earth's first midget, but he is also the first drunken midget in the history of the Earth. The Flying Spaghetti Monster laughs some more at Man's antics. Later, after further drinking, the Flying Spaghetti Monster will create more midgets. Taller midgets that do not share the same name as Man. And he will decree that taller drunken midgets shall never be funnier than shorter drunken midgets. But at this moment in time, there is only Man, his monstrous maker, and the midget's drunken, hilarious impression of a monster who flies and is made out of spaghetti.

THE BLACK SLEEVE OF DESTINY

by Stephen Graham Jones

Dick finds the hoodie on a different rack from the rest. Not that he's even looking, really, but not like he's going to hang out in Used Bras with his mom. He doesn't want to touch the hoodie, either; after forced Goodwill sessions, his hands always smell like formaldehyde. But this hoodie, Dick's already reaching for it before he can stop himself. Just with the back of his finger at first, like hello.

Hello.

His mom throws it in with all of her wonderful finds and then they're ducking back out into the bright, bright day.

By the end of the week, the hoodie makes it up from the utility to Dick's room. Now it smells like mountain spring detergent.

Dick—Richard if he had the choice, or Rick, Ricky, hell, even *Detective*—Dick huddles in his headphones and watches the hoodie, pretending to interrogate it from his place on the bed. Waiting for it to make the first move, here.

Where his mom's left it is draped across the back of his desk chair. Like Dick's name, the chair's a hand-me-down, like he's standing at the bottom of the family hill, all this unasked-for history snowballing down onto him.

Thanks, Dad.

As for the hoodie itself, it's black of course, but somehow not that stupid athletic shade of black. This shade of black's better. Dick can't really explain it, just knows that the vagueness of this particular black, it was what drew him to that one rack in the first place. And of course there's no decal or insignia or corporate affiliation on front, back, or down along the waist. It's the kind of generic that feels intentional, that feels paid for at some place in the mall, except Dick wouldn't be caught stealing there.

His only fear about the hoodie is that Sammy at work is going to like it too. The way it doesn't advertise. The way it isn't crude. The way it's just functional.

Sammy's approximately eighty years old, if not more, but he's still bagging groceries alongside Dick.

Sammy's a kid's name, too.

It's Dick's that's supposed to be for the senior citizens.

The world's so upside down.

Next shift (it's October) Dick discovers why the hoodie was only two dollars: it's a factory second. The right arm's a whole hand longer than the left.

Dick's whole shift, he's constantly chocking that sleeve up, trying to keep it out of the way.

There's a hook in the back of the breakroom nobody

uses. The shirts there are from ten years ago, a whole different style.

This is where Dick plans to retire the hoodie. Let it gather that fine coating of dust on the shoulders, become part of the scenery, part of the museum of uselessness this place already is.

But then, on state-mandated break, standing out by the dumpsters, Dick lowers his cigarette hand down along his leg—learned behavior, keeping your habit on the sly—and that long sleeve falls down over it, swallows his whole hand, so that now there's smoke along his arm, that wonderful heat near his palm, but no cigarette. Just a black sleeve rising to Dick's mouth every twenty seconds or so, for him to breathe from.

It's excellent. The coolest thing all day, all week.

Dick rocks on his heels, forward to his toes, and pulls that invisible cigarette to his mouth again, drags deep. Holds it in.

That night at the carwash by the grocery store, the one that sells vanilla in plastic bottles, straight up from Mexico (it's Dick's mom's birthday), Dick's talking to Catressa at the counter when he becomes aware that he's leaning on the display by her register. The impulse bin, that last-chance spread of junk before you pay out.

Without even having to think about it, one of the turquoise and silver lighters is up his hollow cuff, gulped into his extra hand of sleeve.

Talking to Catressa the whole time, of course. Eye contact and everything, the sleeve moving almost on its own, like an elephant trunk, just without the obvious rest of the elephant.

Dick buys his plastic bottle of vanilla with the rooster on the label and slopes across the parking lot. Never questions how the lighter's gone from his sleeve to his pocket already.

Where else *would* it go?

The next week he wears the hoodie every day. His mom even goes so far (for her) as to compliment him on it. Compliments her purchase, anyway. The bargain she got for him.

Thanks, Mom. Gee.

Bagging old wenches' cat food is the sweetest revenge, now. He can picture them unloading their daily haul in their Harvest Gold kitchens. *Did I not get those mints Alfred likes? But it's on the receipt. Dear, dear. And what about—what about that denture cream, now. Did it fall out in the car?*

Go look, Dick tells them.

It's a good life.

And the mints and cream and medications, they just go up his sleeve, are gone, Dick doesn't care where, but he knows better than to ditch them in the trash under the register, or to try to reshelve them, or to get busted leaving with them. If his assistant manager makes him strip down one fine day, he'll be squeaky. Insulted, even.

He's already practicing making that face, like the world's just confirming everything he suspected.

And—What about Sammy, right? Have you looked at him for this? He could actually use some of this old-lady stuff, couldn't he?

Motive right there. Opportunity everywhere.

It'll be perfect.

Nevermind that some of those nights, his shift over, his shows cycled down, his games beat again, he'll wake with a mint-flavored chalkiness in his mouth, or with his teeth glued together, or just sick, throwing up purple and pink pills for ailments he's not due for for another fifty years.

But it's worth it.

Just to see if he can, Dick stretches the cuff of the hoodie out while stocking, until the elastic's nothing, doesn't remember its own shape. Then he lowers it over a romance paperback when it comes down the Black Belt of Doom.

Like usual, he continues the motion everybody, cameras included, expects, stuffing his hand down into the brown paper bag as if positioning the book to protect the eggs or someshit, and of course—why not?—when his hand comes back up, it's empty. Ready for the next item, already being scanned.

That night, though, Dick wakes up crying, but happy too, the bitter aftertaste of a happy ending in his mouth.

He sits up, touches the tears on his cheek, and laughs at himself.

The next morning, the elastic cuff's back to normal.

Dick would expect nothing less.

"Are you ever going to wash that thing?" Dick's mom asks from her place on the couch, Dick slouching past, doing his best shadow act.

Part of that's having his hood up. Hiding inside it. Just slashing his eyes out at this, that. Them.

"He's going to marry it."

This from Dick's little sister, Gloria. A completely normal name for a complete freak of a humanoid.

Dick's gone.

After school he grabs the bus to the store, begs an extra shift (shuffling, no eye contact: "my mom's birthday"). The assistant manager is proud, impressed, can see Dick's future spread out before both of them.

Dick wonders if the assistant manager's head would fit up the sleeve of a hoodie.

"What's so funny there, sport-o?"

Nothing, Sammy. Just move along, move along.

Sunday everybody's in the store. Like a hurricane's coming. Or zombies. Wrong: another stupid football game. Busy busy. No stocking, just bagging, bagging, like working an assembly line, building the perfect fan from nacho chips and beer.

After a record stretch of abstinence—afraid taking some of those small jars of cheese dip might make him all rah-rah and brainless—Dick lets a slick package of condoms slide back up the heel of his hand, fade up his sleeve. It's a joke. Except:

"Hey, um, yeah. Think I saw that, *Dick*."

It's Bruce. From school. Since second grade. One of the main reasons Dick can't just be Richard.

Tittering in place beside Bruce, his girlfriend Rylene. Complete with pom-poms for some reason. Eating a Dorito from the bag she's not supposed to have already opened. But the rules don't apply, etc.

"Dick?" Tamara the Checkout Queen asks, popping the gum in her mouth like she can, and always does. Staring past that empty sound at Dick.

"Oh, right, right," Bruce says, getting his momentum now that Tanya's tuned in, "forgot who I was talking to. They're like actual clothes for you, right? Raincoat... dick? What was I thinking."

Rylene: crunch, laugh, crunch.

Tanya: pop, pop, giggle.

Dick: nothing intelligible.

In his right hand, though, unasked for, is the small knife he lifted from the carwash the other day. A version of it, anyway.

This one feels bigger. Sharper. Meant for things.

Not an impulse nab at all, apparently.

Bruce is still saying something too, more of the same, Dick knows the tone, the timbre (*up through the chin, under the tongue, where there's no bone*), but just as the blade gleams out from the shadow of Dick's sleeve—or, is the sleeve retracting on its own, like foreskin?—Sammy's there with his twenty-five years of experience, stepping between, avoiding a scene. Showing Queen Tanya how to scroll through the receipt, then—for modesty—going to pull another box of condoms himself, instead of whispering for them over the PA.

Thanks, Dick doesn't say.

Thanks, Bruce *should* be saying.

What Rylene leaves for Dick to remember them by is one of her red pom-pom streamers, winding down into the Black Belt of Doom.

Dick reaches forward, covers the sensor, stops the Belt from pulling the streamer any deeper into the guts of the store.

Nothing clatters from his sleeve.

Two nights later he wakes with a condom on. He peels it off and there's another, and another, twelve in the pack.

Underneath them all he's shriveled, bloodless, strangled.

"Honey?" his mom asks through the bathroom door. "Are you crying?"

Dick doesn't answer.

At lunch he cuts school, heads back to the Goodwill. Wanders the racks.

There's no more factory seconds. The hoodie was the only one.

He scopes the vases and cookware aisle, just hiding mostly, then lowers his hand to a fork with a bamboo handle.

Before he can stop himself, it's his. Gone.

This is closing the circle, he tells himself.

He says it again that afternoon, eating early lasagna in his room with the bamboo fork. That this is it, that it's over.

It even sounds like a lie to him.

At real dinner later that night Dick's mom stabs her hand across the table, to flick Dick's hood back.

This results in the usual amount of yelling and grounding and spaghetti floating through the air.

Thoroughly grounded, Dick sits in his room the next two days—school, home; school, home—finally reaches a hand up to the zipper at his throat, tugs down.

He's not surprised that the teeth are jammed into each other.

It's going to take some speed to pull them apart. Some momentum.

Reverse screw, captain. We're rising, coming up for air.

Dick smiles, jerks the zipper up, and, instead of sticking, it's like it's been waiting for him to do just that: it bites him in the neck.

In the mirror nearly covered with band stickers, Dick can see the slow trickle of blood feeling down along the zipper's thousand-switchback path. And then he gets involved peeling an oval sticker of a band that's on the radio too much now.

When he comes back to his red zipper, it's not red anymore. Surprise, surprise.

Because grounding Dick from work would be like punishing Sammy, too—this is actually Dick's argument, for which he does immediate mental penance, fifty lashes to the cerebellum, thank you, sir—Dick's mom lets him take the Corolla in through the rain.

The kitchen smells like vanilla. The alcohol in it real and pungent.

Gloria watches Dick all the way out the door. Dick watches her back, wishes her well; she'll be the first taste-tester of the afternoon, will have to gauge what's in her mouth against their mom's hopes, will have to either choke down slice after slice to the tune of network gameshows or spend the evening in her room, for being a little liar.

Dick knows.

The Corolla's a stick, and the tires keep chirping on the wet asphalt with first gear, at least the way Dick does it.

Because it's just a Wednesday, Dick's the only one on duty.

But there's a mystery to be solved, too.

Evidently.

Sammy strolls through the automatic doors in his old man raincoat, shakes the mist off his umbrella and asks Money-Order Rhonda if he can deposit this with her?

"Customer's always right," she tells him, taking the umbrella by the handle.

It's their usual disgusting thing. Dick would call it flirting, except it's the kind between a grandfather and his step-granddaughter, something creepy like that.

And then Sammy's whistling up the aisles, just another shopper.

And of course—just one register open—soon enough Dick's standing alongside Tamara as she pop-pops her gum and chats Sammy up.

What comes down the Black Belt of Doom, too: Dick knows immediately that this is a sting operation.

It's cigarettes from Sammy's own pocket, already documented somehow (receipts, photographs, special marks on the wrappers), it's little corn-stabbers, it's turkey thermometers that already look like a joke happening. It's gum and a USB adapter and every other small, easy-to-miss thing Sammy could find that wouldn't fall through the bottom of his basket.

Dick nods about each of them, processes them past, into their separate bags (perishable, non-, household, automotive, office), and the only time—he's promised himself, after all, knows exactly what Sammy's doing—he doesn't feel the item fill its space in the bag, it's one of the travel packets of shampoo. The ones shaped exactly like ketchup packets.

Or, no: mayonnaise.

Dick smiles, could have a plan here, if he wanted.

But no, no.

He shakes his arm as if his sleeve's caught, feels the tiny impact below his hand.

Mystery solved, Sammy? he says with his eyes, and then carries the bags out to the car, lines them up in the trunk like corpses.

The next day it's still raining, somehow.

Sammy's waiting when Dick clocks in.

With the assistant manager.

Before Dick can object, that he didn't take a thing, Sammy holds his hand up.

Between his ancient thumb and pruned forefinger is the turquoise and silver lighter.

"Got left in my shopping bag," Sammy says, almost like a question. Except it's not.

"A gift for the more loyal customers?" the assistant manager asks.

"Was wondering where that went," Dick says, eyes all the way averted.

"If you're wondering," Sammy says, a definite glint in his eyes, "your little girlfriend next door's been called in special, to see if she remembers this purchase. Or if she doesn't."

Dick sucks his cheeks in.

"She's not my girlfriend," he says.

"Either way," the assistant manager says—stubby tie, short-sleeved all-business shirt, the gut always stained with blue ink, from the egg boxes he insists everybody's too thoughtless with—"you either stole it while you were visiting, which is like her stealing it herself, or she sold a minor paraphernalia for tobacco products."

"Maybe I was camping," Dick says.

"Camping," Sammy says, tossing the lighter across.

It traces a perfect arc through the storeroom.

Dick's hand rises to meet it.

The sleeve anyway.

Eye contact with Sammy the whole slow time.

The four-hour shift grinds by. Two bagboys aren't needed, but Sammy's there anyway, whistling to himself when the customers aren't around. Some sick melody not heard by humans for fifty years or more, until now.

"What's her name, that one at the carwash?" Sammy asks once.

Dick flips him off. In his head.

Instead of bagging, he's sweeping. Has to take the padded mats of all six registers out back, blow them out with the hose then hang them over the safety rail to dry.

Two cigarettes later, he's slouched back in, the rain beaded on the black shoulders of his hoodie, a thousand tiny droplets, the world captured in each of them.

There's trash to be hauled out, spills to be mopped, soup to be counted and (re)tagged.

An hour shy of ten—clock-out—Dick plays the mom-card: she's making a cake, it's her birthday, Gloria has to go to bed early.

The assistant manager spins once on his metal stool, considering, and it's finally a financial decision, Dick knows: that's one less hour of minimum wage to pay-out at the end of the week.

"She never knew, either," Dick says, shrugging the hood up over his head.

"Cat?" the assistant manager asks.

Catressa, yes.

Dick says it with his eyes, mostly.

The assistant manager spins halfway back around, is already studying something on his desk.

"She'll make a good waitress somewhere," he says as goodbye, then his whole massive frame chuckles.

On the way out, Dick runs his hand along the label-edge of the condiments shelf, shifting all the prices one item over. Sometimes two.

His other hand balled tight in his sleeve, where no one can see.

One hour and nine minutes later—the car not late *yet*, Mom—Sammy's got the headlights off, is idling at the fire curb by the cart corral, where the squeaky wheeled go to die their slow public deaths.

The air's grey, is at least half exhaled smoke.

Waitress my *ass*, Dick's saying to himself every few drags.

The last cigarette he lit was fifty minutes ago. He's not asking where the new ones are coming from anymore, or how they're getting lit.

Off hatred, he knows.

Sixteen years of it already.

Dick smiles. Starts to rub a port hole in the windshield to see from but realizes at the last moment that that would mean looking at his right hand. So he uses his left, and, instead of a rubbed-clean hole—the defroster sucks—he writes his name backwards, so it'll be readable from the front: D R A H C I R.

No idea why he never thought of that till just this moment.

Or, like he's been saving it for now, yeah.

Like clockwork, then, Sammy ambles out into the night, leaning back to stretch his back, both his hands on his hips.

When he comes down from that stretch, he sees it, what Dick's left: the turquoise and silver lighter.

Just standing there erect on the shiny blacktop.

Sammy cocks his head, takes a careful step forward, then another step, and Dick lowers his—not his hand, but the sleeve, he watches as the long sleeve of the hoodie swallows that five-speed little shifter, deep throating it.

And—more clockwork—the front tires chirp their warning just as Sammy's leaning down for this impossible thing, this lighter, and, because he's old, instead of standing all the way to take the Corolla's impact, he only turns his face to the bright, bright headlights, his shadow thrown so far behind him. Almost as far as he's about to fly.

Dick smiles, but it's so deep in the darkness of his hood that Sammy never sees it.

HOT DOGMA

by Kelli Owen

"Daddy, why is the sky blue?" Jessica smiled at Patrick from the doorway of his home office, eyes wide with anticipation. The raggedy teddy handed down from her mother's childhood swung from her limp grasp.

Patrick smiled. It was time for another round of Jessica's new favorite game—*Why?*

"Well..." He ruffled the blonde curls atop his daughter's head and took a deep breath. "The sun actually gives off a rainbow of colors, but the blue is the one the sky likes the best. The tiny bits and pieces of blue scatters across the clouds better than the others." He watched her purse her lips and contemplate his answer, as he waited for the normal barrage of follow-up questions.

"Okay!" She scampered back to the living room, leaving Patrick to his "silly drawings and naked buildings." Of all the questions Jessica had begun asking, she never asked what an architect was after the initial correction of her pronunciation— "arc-ti-tect-a."

The front door opened and closed with little more than a whisper, but the excited squeal from Jessica let Patrick know April was home. Patrick closed his laptop and the schematics he'd been working on, and followed the sounds of his family to the kitchen.

"Hey hon. How was your day?" He kissed April and pulled Jessica off her mother's leg. "Let Mommy get in the house, honey."

"Not bad for a Monday. Certain clients make me want to legalize public floggings, but a smoke break usually fixes that." She pulled the groceries from the bag in her hand and put them on the counter.

"I thought I was grilling." He eyed the taco seasoning and spaghetti sauce.

"Oh, you are. This is for the rest of the week." She winked at him and nodded toward the sliding glass door to their small patio and the gas grill there.

"Burgers and dogs?"

"You know it."

"Daddy, why do they call them hot dogs?"

"Ah, my little inquisitor, come help Daddy get the grill ready and we'll discover *all kinds* of things about your food you don't want to know."

"Patrick..." April cocked her head to the side.

"I know, I know. Only answer direct questions with the truth, but come on. You do know how disgusting the truth is about hot dogs, right? Plus, it's kind of funny."

"Just be gentle about it. We *do* want her to eat dinner." She leaned over and kissed him again before shooing them out the door to start the grill, so she could put groceries away.

Bedtime was full of seriousness and silliness, as usual. Patrick was convinced Jessica spent her day coming up with new questions to ask. For a four-year-old, he thought she was awfully precocious.

However, April insisted, "First born children are naturally precocious. The second," she patted her slightly swollen belly and indicated the sibling just beginning to kick out at the world, "won't be nearly as curious. Of course, the older child usually provides hours and hours of informative monologue." She smiled and pushed open their daughter's bedroom door. "After you, professor."

"Daddy, where did the cows and chickens go when they became hot dogs?" Jessica began before her parents crossed the threshold.

Oh boy. Patrick looked to April in the doorway. His wife's nod reassured him she'd take this one and he relaxed. He was much more comfortable with the scientific questions.

"Well honey, some people think they go to heaven just like people do." She answered from the doorway.

"Heaven?" Jessica leaned forward and put her chin into the cradle of her tiny hands.

"Some people?" Patrick whispered.

"Yes. Remember… truth and open-ended answers." She winked at him. "Trust me, it's what my mother did."

"Yeah, but you ended up an atheist."

"So? You're only a Christian on Christmas and Easter." She nudged him into the room and returned her attention to Jessica.

"There are a lot of different beliefs about what happens to you when you die. Even your pets—"

"Like Fishy-Face?" Jessica interrupted.

"Yep, like Fishy-Face, or the animals in your hot dog."

"Is it okay if I don't eat hot dogs anymore?" Jessica wrinkled her nose, her bright pink Cupid lips pursed in disgust.

"Sure honey, but I'm betting you'll want another one before the weekend." April sat on the edge of the bed and pulled the blankets up over Jessica.

"Heaven, Mommy…"

"Okay, *some* people think you go to heaven. They say heaven is a wonderful place where you'll see all your family and friends and will always be happy. *Other* people don't believe in heaven. They think you might be a ghost or be born all over again into a new baby's body, or even as an animal."

"Eww, I don't want to be a ghost-born hot dog!" Her tiny blonde brows furrowed in confusion.

"No worries about that, silly." April turned on the small table lamp next to the bed—the silhouettes of Disney characters cast faint beams of hope across the walls to scare away the monsters—and leaned in to kiss Jessica.

"You sure truth is really the best option here?" Patrick watched his daughter's face twist in consideration.

"Always." She used her mommy-means-it voice on Patrick and he raised an eyebrow at her.

"Even when the truth is confusing? It just leads to more questions."

"And this is bad, how? The more she asks, the more she learns." April playfully punched his arm. "Plus, we agreed to this before she was even born."

"I know. I know." He grabbed Jessica's ankles and slid her down her mattress. He tucked her teddy under the blanket with her and kissed her forehead. "Do you want to do prayers tonight?"

"Yes, Daddy. I like it when we whisper to gods."

"Just the one God, honey. Just one." Patrick knelt beside his daughter as April slipped out of the room.

At the doorway April heard her daughter begin the other part of the deal they'd made regarding child rearing—the nightly ritual of prayers. She'd hated agreeing to it at the time, but had developed a fondness for the tender moments Patrick and Jessica shared. Though she'd never admit it to Patrick, she looked forward to prayer time.

"God bless Mommy and Daddy. And Grammas and Grampas and cousin Mary and Teddy Bear." Her voice changed and April was reminded of a pouting Shirley Temple in some movie she couldn't quite place. "And the poor poor hot dogs. Don't let them be reborned into ghost heavens."

April stood outside the door, listening with a grin.

"Daddy. Who's in charge of heaven? Is it the gods? Can they protect the hot dogs?"

"Just one God, honey."

"Ahem." April pretended to cough from the hallway.

Patrick rolled his eyes at the empty doorway. "Well, depending on what you believe in, it might be God. Just the one."

"So there *is* more than one?" The excitement in Jessica's voice mimicked her movements as she sat up in bed, eyes wide even as she yawned.

"It's late, honey." Patrick gently pushed her back down to her pillow and kissed her forehead. "Save some questions for tomorrow."

"Okay, Daddy." She turned to her side and closed her eyes, squeezing her bear. "Night-night, Mommy."

April smiled. Jessica always seemed to know when April was eavesdropping. "Night-night, sweetie."

Patrick turned off the overhead light, exited the room, and quietly shut the door. He turned to April in the dim light of the hallway and gawked at her. "Gods? I don't know, April…"

"Maybe she'll forget by morning." April smirked and walked down the hall toward the living room.

"Daddy, why—"

"Shhh…" Patrick hushed her, pointing to the telephone against his head.

Jessica frowned and plopped down in the doorway of his

office. Patrick wrote down the phone number the recording provided and hung up.

"Sorry, you weren't talking." Jessica didn't look up from the tiny white tennis shoe she studied and Patrick found himself both appreciative of her respecting his work and saddened she felt so bad for interrupting.

"It's okay, honey. I was listening and I'm done now." He walked over and squatted in front of her, gently lifting her head with a single finger under her chin. "What's up, pumpkin?"

Her large blue eyes were shiny with tears and trepidation. Her lower lip quivered as she spoke. "I just wanted to know..." Her voice trailed off and she looked down again.

Patrick scooped her up in his arms. "Honey, you don't have to feel so bad. It's okay, you stopped right away. You know, I interrupt people sometimes, too."

"You do?" She straightened in his arms, her rag doll impression forgotten.

"People do it all the time. Especially when excited about something." He smiled and kissed her forehead. "So what are you all excited about?"

"The hot dogs, Daddy." She wiggled until he put her back down—a mild improvement on her previously vocal demands to be let loose—and scurried down the hall, forcing Patrick to follow her. "When they go to heaven and see the gods and all their family... Do they stay there? Don't they get bored? Do they play games? And why do we only have pictures of the old man god? Where are the other pictures? The other gods?"

Her questions ran together in a breathless cacophony of inquisition. His mouth opened to answer the first but hung slack-jawed as the rest poured from her like salt from a shaker with a loose top, too fast to react. As he exited the hallway into the living room, he thought the hinge of his jaw popped as it lowered further in shock.

The contents of the bookcase next to the television had

been haphazardly scattered about the floor, some books open, some closed, all affected by the curiosity of the Jessica monster.

"Honey…" Patrick's eyebrows lowered, mimicking the corners of his frowning mouth, as he looked at the mess sure to cost him more than a little work time to clean up. "What were you doing?"

"You were busy. I didn't wanna bother you." Her large eyes widened and her lips tightened in a smile meant to project all the innocent cuteness she'd learned to use defensively at four. "I was looking for the gods…"

If Patrick hadn't known better, he'd have thought she expertly batted her eyes at him like some practiced femme fatale. "Jess…" He glanced at the mess on the floor, his family's large leather-bound Bible at the center, opened to the reproduction of Michelangelo's Creation of Adam.

Patrick rolled his eyes and looked at his watch. Half an hour before April would be home, and he really didn't want to tackle this one alone.

"Let's clean this up before Mommy gets home. Then we can talk about all your questions, okay?"

Jessica's gaze moved to follow her father's and her eyebrows raised, as if she hadn't realized what kind of mess she'd made until that moment. "Okay, Daddy." She bent and reverently picked up the heavy Bible with a grunt and moved it to the coffee table. "I wanna keep this one out."

In an organized flurry, the two of them reshelved the books—Jessica handing them to Patrick and him placing them on the appropriate shelf, albeit not necessarily in the order they were in previously. They were almost done when April walked in the door.

Dropping her purse on the small table near the door and kicking her shoes toward the closet, April looked quizzically at the two of them on the living room floor.

"I was looking for the gods, Mommy, but I only found the

one that looks like Grampa. Do they all look like Grampa?" Jessica jumped up from her position on the floor and ran to embrace her mother's leg.

"Yeah, one of *those* days." Patrick flashed his teeth in a feigned smile.

"Pizza?" April picked up Jessica and squeezed her, speaking over the child's shoulder.

"Yeah, I'll order it. You can field questions…" He picked up the last three books and set them on the top of the case. "And the bevy that will come flying out after it." He pulled his phone from his pocket and was already dialing before entering the kitchen.

"Grandpa, huh?" April walked to the couch and sat down with Jessica on her lap facing her.

"Yeah. He's really old. See, Mommy?" Jessica twisted toward the table and pointed at the open page of the Bible.

"Ahh, yes. That god is usually shown to be old. *Old* means *wise*, you know? That's why Grandma and Grandpa know all those things they know."

"So all the gods are old?"

"Well…" April thought about it for a moment. "No. I guess they're not. The Romans, Greeks, some of the Asian gods… No, gods can be almost any age I guess."

"Do we have pictures of them all?"

April looked at the bookcase, cocking her head slightly to more easily see titles on the spines. "Hmmm, doesn't look like it. I must have gotten rid of those books after college." She looked back to Jessica's disappointed pout. "We could look them up on Daddy's computer if you want."

"Yeah!"

April stood up, lifting Jessica with her, and headed toward Patrick's home office. "Using your Google, honey." She spoke into the kitchen as they walked past.

"Pizza's ordered," he announced while following them.

While they waited for dinner to be delivered, they looked at pictures of gods and fielded question after question from Jessica. The Internet image search proved to be just as helpful as it was hurtful in Patrick's opinion. April thought it was funny because of the range of gods and images tagged as such—cartoons, satirical newspaper comics, anime, and a plethora of uploaded visualizations made them both happy the "safe search" feature had been turned on before they started.

"That god has too many arms."

"That one's an elephant!"

"Why is that one *green?*"

The questions continued until several pages in when Jessica stopped pointing and just stared at the screen. April started to scroll down only to be halted by a tiny hand on her arm and an excited voice.

"Wait, Mommy! Go back up…"

April went back to the top of the page.

"Yeah, there. What is *that?* That can't be a god, that's just gaspetti!" Jessica giggled.

"That's the Flying Spaghetti Monster, honey." April smiled at Patrick, who frowned in response.

"So it *is* gaspetti?"

"No, that god just *looks* like spaghetti."

"That's not a real god, though, April." Patrick interjected.

"Isn't it?" April countered. "Remember, we explain them all and she decides who's real and who isn't."

"Why are there so many?" Jessica interrupted her parents.

"Different people, in different places, all believe different things." April stroked Jessica's hair.

"And most of the people that live here believe in the one that looks like Grandpa." Patrick pushed an extra vote for his beliefs to April's chagrin and was treated to the evil eye for his efforts.

"But how do they know which one?" Jessica was oblivious

to her parents' muted argument.

"Most just believe what their parents believe. But we promise to always tell you *all* the options and let *you* decide what sounds best for you, okay?" April spoke in a soothing tone, belying her anger at Patrick's attempt to sway Jessica.

"But how will I know? Can I like them all?"

"Yes you can. Or none if that's what you'd prefer." April snarled at Patrick as she spoke, her antagonistic response to his subtle push obvious only to him.

"That might be confusing." Patrick could see there was no winning the argument and tried to move the conversation forward. "You don't have to decide right now, honey. You probably won't decide until you're much older."

The doorbell rang, announcing dinner's arrival in thirty minutes or less, and offering a reprieve to the questions. Patrick spun away from the computer. "Thank God," he said, and immediately regretted his choice of words as he left the room. "Dinner's here. Close that and come eat," he called from the hallway, pulling his wallet from his back pocket to pay the delivery boy.

Dinner was free of questions. Jessica remained quiet during their bedtime routine and into the next day. After two whole days without any further questions on gods or any other topics, Patrick started to worry they'd filled her head with too much.

"She's too young to grasp everything we can offer her. Shouldn't we dumb it down to a few choices and expand over time?"

April disagreed with his assessment, "She's a lot smarter than you realize. Kids usually are. They say you can teach children under four multiple languages and they take to them much easier than older children and adults. She's a sponge. Let her absorb what she can."

While they discussed it off and on, Jessica remained stoic. Patrick almost missed the game of *Why?* April assured him it would return. "She's just processing it all. After all, she saw everything from Kali to *Calvin and Hobbes* in under half an hour."

Almost a full week after the night of the gods, Jessica's questions resumed on a more cautious level. "Daddy, why do they say delivery boy but sometimes it's a girl?"

Patrick smiled, relieved at the simplicity of the topic and happy to have his little inquisitor back. He spent the afternoon working on a draft for an expansion to the hospital's rear wing, and happily answering questions posed to him from his office doorway.

Jessica ran to greet her mother as usual. By the time Patrick finished his work ten minutes later and joined them, Jessica was sitting on the counter. She watched her mother cook, and told April everything she'd learned in a run-on sentence of excited chatter.

"Hmmm... smells good." He kissed April before eyeballing the pan on the stove. "Oh, meat sauce or meatballs?"

"Meatballs, my dear." She smiled, "That prefab package of Italian meatballs you like was on sale."

As she dropped the spaghetti into the large pot of water, the previous week's conversations with her daughter came back to April and she paused. Jessica didn't seem to be connecting the two things, and Patrick furrowed his eyebrows at her for a moment, unsure what she was insinuating with her single raised eyebrow. His face relaxed into an expression of understanding and he glanced at Jessica as well. He shrugged to April, neither of them saying a word, and both presuming Jessica had moved on to other things and forgotten all about the various gods they'd shown her.

"Why isn't parmi-john mushy like other cheeses?" Jessica queried from her booster seat as April filled plates. The child's nose wrinkled up as she studied the cheese shaker in front of her.

"It's considered a hard cheese, honey. Some cheeses are harder than others, or can dry like this. Some are really wet and don't dry but will crumble when you use them on things." Patrick put a glass of milk in front of Jessica and sat across from her with his own plate.

April put the colorful toddler plate of spaghetti in front of Jessica and snapped her *big-girl bib* into place. "Like Grandma puts on her salads. Those lumpy bits of white are a wet cheese."

"Oooh… okay." Jessica smiled and picked up her fork.

Poised above one of the two pieces of halved meatballs on her plate, Jessica's fork stopped in midair. The sauce rolled lazily down the side of the meatball, like an eyelid closing, and her face wrinkled up in concern.

Jessica's eyes squinted and a tiny noise came from her pursed lips. April looked over in time to see Jessica's bottom lip begin to quiver. Patrick looked up at the clatter of Jessica's fork being dropped to the table. They exchanged a hesitant glance.

"Hon?" April questioned as she picked up the fork to hand back to Jessica.

"He winked at me…" Her voice was small, as if she'd been scolded. "God winked at me."

"Jessica, that's not God—" Patrick began but April's head snapped in his direction, eyes wide in a silent threat, stopping him. He motioned a pantomimed "What?" at her.

April shook her head and mouthed, *Don't make it worse.*

They remained locked in a stare, both trying to figure out the best course of action. April nodded affirmation of an idea.

"But your spaghetti isn't flying, honey. It's just spaghetti."

"Birds don't always fly, Mommy. They have to rest and sleep and stuff…" She looked up. "Daddy said so. Didn't you, Daddy?

"Well yeah, but that's birds. Not a god." He swallowed, uncomfortable with his own words but following April's lead.

"But he winked at me!" Jessica pushed the plate away from her and fell forward, her head flopping onto her arms on the table. "I can't eat god! I can't! Or I'll never go to heavens and play games." She sobbed, occasionally wailing unintelligibly.

Patrick looked at April. "Well, genius?"

April huffed quietly, still certain their decision almost five years beforehand had been the right one, but suddenly questioning the timing of full truths versus maturity of the subject matter. Her shoulders slumped in resignation and she patted Jessica's back.

"Honey… Jess…"

Jessica looked up at her mother, the alligator tears of childhood causing snot to run freely from her nose. She sniffled and pouted at her mother.

"I want a hot dog."

EXTRA LIVES

by Jess Gulbranson

"What were your parents like?" This was uncomfortable. Matt knew that it was supposed to be a casual coffee date, but this girl was intense. She leaned in across the little table from the huge overstuffed chair, green eyes and freckles all he could see.

"You'll never believe this," he said. "I don't normally talk about it. But they were fundies."

She crooked her mouth in a way that instantly began giving him wood. *Don't freak out*, he thought. *Don't stress. It's about boner management.* But she was intense, her eyes had him on lockdown, so she wasn't looking at his package anyway. "Fundies, huh? You seem pretty normal. Almost buttoned down, if you don't mind me saying so. Aren't you fundie kids usually crazy from rebelling?"

"No mohawk here. Yeah, I am pretty normal. But it's the opposite of what you're thinking. My parents were fundie Pastafarians." He was blushing. She brought her mug of chai up a little too quickly to stifle some laughter, and spilled some on her upper lip and dropped the mug. Now she was laughing. He blushed some more and got up to grab some napkins.

When he came back to the table and started mopping up

153

the spill, she had composed herself. Mostly. "I'm so sorry to laugh," she said, and gave him that crooked smile. Oh man, did he love redheads. "But it makes sense, what you said. I mean, to rebel against that you must have really toed the line."

"Yeah, first thing I did was go out and get my business degree, and got a job as a comptroller at Yoyodyne. You can't spell 'dumbass' without 'MBA', though and once I got a little older I bailed."

She had leaned a little closer to him, and was leaning over the huge armrest of the chair. "I can't imagine what you were like as a little boy." Matt sighed.

"It wasn't easy. I mean, when I was *little* little, it was cool, but even when I was like seven or eight I started to figure out how fucking weir—excuse me, how weird it was. My moms were hardcore. We didn't just do the church on Sunday thing, but a couple of times throughout the week I had to go the Pastinis-the youth club- while my moms went to small group discussion. We had to wear these little pirate hats and memorize verses. If we were lucky there'd be time left over to play kickball."

"You poor thing." She poked him hard in the ribs, but as she was pulling back she left her hand on his knee. *Boner management*, he thought.

"That's not even the worst. We had a big shrine in the kitchen—well, technically it was the stove, but my mom Patty went a little ape with the JB Weld and little noodle-shaped metal bits. It looked like a steampunk version of some little kid's—some *normal* little kid's—kindergarten art project. I couldn't bring any of my friends home from school, it was just too weird. They didn't even talk normally, it was always 'appendage' this and 'noodly' that." Matt paused there. "I'm sorry, listen to me go. You probably didn't come tonight to listen to me carp about my messed-up childhood."

"It's fascinating. And you're cute when you're blushing." Which set his face crimson again. "We don't have to talk about it if you're too embarassed," she said. Then, with a mischievous look in her eyes, she squeezed his knee. "Wait—just one more thing. What was the absolute craziest thing that ever happened to you when you were at home?"

"When my moms got arrested." He put his hand on top of hers. This was going better than he'd hoped.

"I have got to hear this," she said. "How did your parents get arrested?"

"They shot a cannon at some ninjas."

"What! No way. How did that happen?" Her eyes were wide and he was glad she didn't have any more chai, because she looked like she was about to lose it again.

"When I was in high school there was a big ninja pride parade down on the waterfront, and that was something the Fundie Pastafarians could *not* abide, so of course they had to protest. With signs and stuff at first, but it started to get a little out of hand and my mom Marian fired the cannon. Nobody got hurt of course, because the cannon was loaded with limp—"

"Fettucini?" she ventured.

"Acini de pepe, actually, but you get the picture."

She rubbed his knee some. "That sucks. At least nobody was hurt. Did they go to jail? You seem like the kind of responsible kid who'd end up bailing his parents out."

"Nah, luckily not. They got as far as the back of the squad car, you know those crazy plastic seats with a little niche for the handcuffs. The cop happened to be a Zen Buddhist, so he let them off with just a warning, and a really stern koan. Plus he made me promise to keep them out of trouble."

"Did you?"

"No, I went to live with my uncle Ryan not long after that." She gave him a real smile, sincere.

"You want to get out of here? It's perfect weather to take a walk." She was already putting her red hair back in a tie, so he took a quick swig of his coffee.

"I would love to. You're right..." Matt looked out the window through the gaps in the mauve window shades. It was a beautiful fading light, he knew the air was cooling down. He looked over at her and smiled. He hadn't had a date play out like this since high school.

They got up and walked out of the little coffee shop, and he didn't even respond to the baristas as they all said goodbye. Out on the street, his predictions were confirmed, and he unbuttoned the jacket in which he was perhaps a touch overdressed. She glanced at him as he did so and he tried not to be self-conscious. They started walking down the street, it was a cute little district full of antique stores that operated out of historic buildings.

For a moment it was like just after they had ordered coffee-no words at all, and they didn't look at each other. Then Matt summoned up a little bit of courage and reached over to take her hand. Doing it blind led him to snag her bracelet first, but then he slid down and held her hand. She squeezed his back.

"It's been a weird thing, growing up early. Or I think so. Maybe parts of me never grew up, not like they should have."

She nodded. "I was so close to having the American dream nuclear family, but it all skewed early. My brother died of leukemia when he was eleven—I was only a few years older than him. My mom and dad were already pretty far apart when that happened, and when Bill died it was just worse. She was the classic workaholic, always traveling and working late at the office. My dad was a stay-at-home, he was a sculptor. So he was always there for us, but after Bill died I think he started to enjoy playing himself off against my mom, playing the martyr and whatever." She held his hand a little tighter and sighed. "It was essentially true. My mom was a real bitch. The only thing that was ever really wrong with my dad was that he had this unreasonable expectation that I was going to grow up to be a famous sculptor like him."

"So you grew up to be a stockbroker."

"Nope. A sculptor." They looked at each other for a moment as they stood at a crosswalk. She leaned over and gave him a kiss on the cheek. "You've got me thinking, though. What if you grew up in a house that had a different religion? How different would you be."

Matt nodded, though what proposition he was confirming he didn't know. "I can't imagine anything else, you know. Even when I went to live with Uncle Ryan, everything was still a reaction to the church and what it stood for. I was always not doing things because they would, or vice versa."

"Yeah. You know, it was funny when you mentioned that cop. My dad was a Buddhist too. He used to really want us to think about how shitty things were getting, with Bill, or the divorce, and then decide to be happy anyway. Which seemed retarded at the time, and I distinctly remember telling him to go to hell—oops, I mean, wherever it is bad Buddhists go. But he meant well."

"I've been pretty happy since I left home, with nothing." They had passed the knot of stores in this neighborhood, and were starting to get into some residential. The houses were much the same, but if anything a little quirkier in their decoration.

"Me too," she said. "But do you ever question that? Like there might be more?"

He smiled at her. "My moms ran an independent bookstore. Of course I do."

She was laughing again. "Nice. Do you know what time it is?" She started to fumble in her purse for her phone.

"It's almost eight. Do you need to get home? We can head that way if you... want to." *Damn*, he thought.

"Oh no, honey. You signed on for a date with me, I've got you all night." *What*. She gave him the crooked grin again, and turned into him as they stopped. "Okay, look, this is completely crazy. But, just shut up for a second while I explain myself, or you're going to think I've lost it."

"Okay."

"So, I used to go out with this guy, a real hipster. He didn't do anything that wasn't ironic. As soon as he realized that all the cool kids he knew were atheists, he decided to start going to church really seriously. Like, he obviously didn't believe in it—and it was completely ridiculous—but that's how hipsters are."

"I wouldn't know." He was smiling even though he was a little concerned at where this was going. Mentioning old boyfriends was never good at the early-evening-stroll phase of a date.

"Don't even get me started on the music he listened to or the hats he wore. Or the mustaches. Let's just say I didn't go out with him for very long."

"Let's."

"Okay, so he did all the usual churches, and boy did I get dragged along to some lame worship services. I hope I never see a female backup singer again. Anyway, not long before I broke up with him he had started going to this really weird place." There was a pause, and he let her continue like she had asked. "I think we should go, tonight. Not seriously, but just for kicks. Like, watch "Plan 9" kicks. What do you think?"

He hesitated. "Just... how weird? Bit by poisonous snakes weird?"

"As weird as you can get without getting bitten by a snake or married in a mass ceremony. Mostly harmless."

"Uh huh. Well, as first dates go, this one has been a doozy. I don't want it to end. I'm game!"

"That's my boy. Let's catch a bus."

There was one that ran down this avenue and luckily it ran every fifteen-ish minutes, so before they had waited a couple of minutes it was bearing down on them. Matt paid—she had insisted on going dutch with the coffee, but he had to sneak in some old-fashioned chivalry somewhere. Yet another aversion of his family history. She was suitably appreciative, holding his hand as they scooted unsteadily to the back of the bus as it lurched off down the street.

"How far is this place?" he asked. "Not that it matters, I mean. Just curious."

"Uh, it's down toward the end of Barron. So, what, five minutes?" Matt nodded.

"Fair enough. Now, you wouldn't be leading me into something, well, really weird would you? This better not be some crazy left field conversion ploy."

"Do you really think that?" She leaned back. There was some indignation—feigned or not, Matt was confused that she could look so appealing with such a dramatic frown on her face. He was ready to backpedal if necessary. That would not be a problem. And it turned out not to be one anyway. Her smile returned from whatever phantom zone it had been banished to temporarily—feigned or not.

"Nope. No way. Just, uh…" he coughed and dropped his voice to a much lower and more gravely octave. "CONVERSATION. Ehhhh… ." She giggled.

"Good. You want the surprise spoiled?" He nodded, and she leaned back in the bus seat and peered out the window, trying to figure out how long the bus had. *Hello cleavage*, Matt thought, and quickly averted his eyes when she turned back toward him. "Picture a regular cult sect whatever, but really trying hard to do things wrong. No, not wrong. What word am I looking for… hard. Really really difficult to make sense of. Like, Nintendo hard." Her mouth curled up in a devious smile, and clearly there was some part of what she was saying was a joke he wasn't in on. But that smile… *If she isn't careful I'm going to be Nintendo hard*, he thought.

"Wow. Okay, I'll just let it sink in when we get there, then. So you're probably setting me up for some stage show participation thing, like I'm a Rocky Horror version."

"What would you do if I did, a nice Pastafarian boy like you?"

"Whatever you'd let me…"

She responded by pulling the plastic cord to signal their bus stop. It responded with a ding, and they both got up as the bus slowed. Standing just as close as they had been sitting in the coffee shop. She smelled like… patchouli?

They stepped onto the street, and with a great wheeze the bus's door closed and it took off. They were on another street, in a neighborhood that was residential tending toward industrial. *Split zoning*, Matt thought. *Nice place for a church.* "This is it," she said. 'It', in this case, was a disappointingly boxy and gray little warehouse-type building.

"Hmm." There wasn't much to recommend this place as an outre spiritual experience. Or any kind of experience. It looked like the kind of building that had a business in it, like plastic injection moulding or something, but you never saw anyone enter or anyone leave. There was a quiet sense of failure around it, and a couple of other similar buildings on the block that Matt could see with a quick double turn of his head.

What wasn't quiet was something in the back. A deep bass throb reached its muffled way through the building. Matt knew that sound. His best friend growing up, Blake, had been in a band, and Matt had sat through enough concerts to know a few things. The drummer showed up before anyone else, set up, and then left until it was time. The bass player was always there not long after, and he would stand on the stage, by himself, picking and plucking expectantly. The guitarist would show up five minutes before the show was due to start, and you'd be lucky if the singer showed up at all. It was like a universal rule, or some goofy archetype.

So Matt and his date were to be treated to a worship band. Great.

"It's around the back," she said. As they stepped onto the concrete strip that went around the corner toward the back of the building, Matt noticed a small sign underneath the brass address numerals on the front of the building: IMANOK CONGREGATION, in BACK. The sign looked to have been printed on a cheap-ass laser printer. Ten years ago.

Matt took her hand and let her lead the way. The back entrance was open, and held stairs down a basement area. In front of the opening, the bass sound had a lot more definition, and it was as he had expected—the sound of a bass player standing there like a dumbass, noodling around. He was seriously having high school flashbacks now.

Down in the basement there was more noise, but most of it was muted conversation. Here was the big surprise. The people here, the congregation, he supposed, was the most diverse group he had ever seen. No, 'diverse' was being overly charitable. These people were fucking weird. Closest to him was a tall, scrawny ginger in a fetid leather hat and a black shirt—well, black everything—a black shirt emblazoned with a white gothic script that said VAMPIRE. This jasper was talking to an old lady in what passed for hippie clothing these days. Near them was a set of twin girls, probably in their twenties, dressed like a couple of sexy peppermints. They were talking with a beturbanned businessman in a suit with a very bright red tie.

"This way," she said, clasping his hand a little tighter and dragging him toward the back of some clearly stolen pews. The basement church was a lot bigger than it looked from the outside, like some cheesy science fiction joke. And the congregation was a lot weirder the more he looked at it. It wasn't just their outfits ("costumes," his mother Elly would have called them) or the variety of people. The atmosphere—as evidenced by glazed eyes and uncanny valley facial expressions—was just fucking weird. The bass player kept noodling, and Matt refrained from looking at him, out of a sense of shared embarrassment.

His date leaned back—*Hello cleavage*—let her red hair out of its confines, dangling down toward her chair back, before tying it back up again. She looked at him. "So, I don't know if it will actually happen, but if they decide to ask you questions or something, I'd probably not mention the... noodle thing."

What. "Not that I had any plan to anyway. But, um, thanks for the warning." Some more musicians had come up on stage. A keyboardist and a chick backup singer. How typical. No sign of any sort of clergy, at least that he could see, but the crowd was clearly responding to something, and they began sitting down. "So..."

"Shh!" She cut him off. "Here comes the guy now!"

And sure as shit, this is pretty much what he would have expected at this point, as the band launched into a limp-dick Christian rock version of "Crazy Train." The priest—or pastor or whatever—came out now in a shuffling gate that seemed to barely hold back some manic energy. He was dressed in a big suit—Matt was momentarily reminded of some David Byrne parody—that seemed to have been assembled out of... dear lord. A power pad. Here and there across the black and white vinyl were the remnants of blue and red As and Bs. His outfit didn't stop there. An orange zapper was holstered at his belt, he was draped from head to foot in various cords, and oh... there it was, from the tips of the fingers on his right hand almost to his elbow. Power Glove. *It's so bad*, Matt whispered to himself, then looked over at his date.

She was grinning, laughing. Enjoying herself a bit too much. Was she one of those people who would put on a bad movie—not like *Plan 9* bad, but *Steel Magnolias* bad—just to have some ironic laughs? Matt had his first real doubts about this date. Was this the kind of girl he could spend the rest of his life with? No matter how hot she was? Still looking at her,

Matt realized he needed to chill and just let whatever was going to happen, happen.

He leaned in and tried to yell over the music. "Wow, now he's playing wit—"

"SHH!" She put her finger to his lips and gave him a more sedate smile. "It's just about to get good," she whispered. "We can go if it's too weird for you." Matt shook his head furiously. He really did want to spend as much time with her as he could.

"WEEEEEEELLLLLCOOOOME BROTHERS AND SISTERS!" The preacher screamed his welcome at a volume just short of distortion. The crowd responded in kind. "And how are all you little chilluns THIS EVENING?" The crowd did it again, but their response to this was as unintelligible as their first outburst.

"Oh shit," his date said, "it's about to get hilarious."

The preacher walked up to the edge of the foot-high stage, and leaned forward at such an exaggerated angle that Matt was afraid he would fall forward and hurt himself. He had thrown his head back at another exaggerated angle and Matt could see his face, or at least as much of it as was visible behind a microphone and some Ray-Bans with florescent pink temple guards.

"Brothers and sisters... can I turn things down now?" The crowd roared in the affirmative, and as it died down the band had switched to a low key "867-5309." "Very well. Now, in the house tonight I notice a few new faces. That's all right. It's never too late to come into the TRUTH!" As he yelled he pumped his Power Gloved fist in the air, and the band responded with a brief musical stab. "And the LIGHT!" The guy had the crowd electrified.

Matt looked at his date. She shrugged, and mouthed *Having fun?* Matt nodded. He put his arm around her.

"There are those who insist that this congregation is a cult.

But I will tell you," and here Matt could swear the preacher was looking at him, "that we have the AN-SWER! All it takes is a little belief. Don't believe me?" The band changed its tune, something playfully melodramatic, but Matt couldn't place it. "Maybe you had faith one time. Maybe you grew up in the bosom of religion. But somewhere along the path it got lost. And now you're miserable!" Now he could place the song. *The Final Countdown, ugh*, he thought. He looked at his date. This was starting to get weird. She shook her head and smiled.

The preacher jumped down off the short stage, and walked up to them. He looked at Matt and his date. "A couple of lovebirds, huh? Here at an evening service for a lark?" Matt and his date turned to each other, hesitant. She grinned and he did too. Then the Power Glove landed in a stout grip on Matt's shoulder. "No worry, brother. Any way to bring some new faces into the fold! As a monastic friend of mine once said, *kusala upaya*! But that's not just it, is it? Can't just start over as a good person in the shine of faith, without some help..."

Matt dared to look the preacher in the face, but the cool shades were unreadable. The preacher looked like a bad dude. Luckily, the Glove left his shoulder and the preacher jumped up on the stage with a very tidy scissor kick. "Come on brothers and sisters! We know life is hard! A mystery in an enigma in a conundrum, all wrapped up tidy in one tough nut to crack! Wouldn't it be easier if there was," he deepened his voice to a theatrical growl, "... a code?" The crowd's response to this was louder and more raucous, and as they went nuts the band switched again, to what sounded like a sleazy game show. Or rather, a specific sleazy game show. Matt could definitely recognize "Family Feud" when he heard it.

"Let's go," he whispered to Sara. She nodded, and he took her hand and whisked her out of the basement as the congregation started going truly apeshit, interspersed with the preacher's cries of "Witness!" and "Testify!" and "GIVE IT TO ME!"

Outside, the noise was greatly muffled. Hand in hand, Matt and Sara walked out to the front walk. Matt leaned in and kissed her. She smelled like patchouli. Her cheeks and forehead were slightly sweaty from being in the stuffy basement. Sara kissed him back, and they wrapped their arms around each other.

In the background, the preacher was still audible, as he led his frenzied congregation in the recital of their holy code.

"Can I get an UP?"

"UP!"

"Brothers and sisters, can I get a DOWN?"

"DOWN!"

"Amen, can I hear you go to the left and rrrrright..."

"LEFT, RIGHT, LEFT, RIGHT!"

"Oh lord, I can feel it brothers and sisters! FROM THE TOP..."

Matt and Sara broke off their kiss and walked down the street, hand in hand, to the bus stop, leaving the preacher and his flock to recite their mantra as one.

"UP! UP! DOWN! DOWN! LEFT! RIGHT! LEFT! RIGHT! B! A! SELECT! START!"

THE HOLY BOWL

by Jeffrey Thomas

I don't blame you for crying. I cried for days when I first came here myself. Don't ask me how many days. As you can see it's impossible to judge the passage of time here. I can't even tell if it's day or night. I don't know how far from my cell the nearest window is. Sometimes when a guard comes to bring my food I can smell that his clothes are warm from the sun. So a window or maybe even a door can't be far. Once I swear I saw a patch of sunlight still clinging to a guard's shoulder before it faded away.

You should come to the bars so I can see you. It might give you a little comfort. I'm sorry for your situation whatever it is but I hate to confess I'm happy to have someone to talk to. I don't know when I last spoke to someone other than the guards or the interrogators. I don't know how long I've been here.

For some time I believed I might be the only prisoner in this place. Actually I believed that right up until I woke up and heard you in your cell. I never hear voices from other prisoners. If people other than me were being interrogated you'd expect to hear them cry out as I do. Or wail in their cells from the pain afterwards. I don't hear other doors slamming above or below or around me except for one big metal door down the hall when someone comes to see me. I was blindfolded when they brought me to my cell. But if there were other men in the cells I passed I'm sure I would have heard them or even smelled them.

When my blindfold came off and I was left here I realized what an old place this is. You can see for yourself. They did take your blindfold off I'm sure. When you're ready you'll look around a bit. I can never see my reflection clearly but I can see enough of me to know I match the surroundings now. These surroundings surprised me when I saw the shape this place is in. I can't see any windows or doors when I get right up to the bars like I am now but I can still see enough of the hallway and the vacant cells. Your cell in particular vexed me. It was so black and empty directly opposite my cell like an open grave waiting for me. Funny that they put you so close to me. It seems too considerate to give me company after the way they've treated me otherwise.

So you'll know what to expect I can fill you in on things I've had to learn on my own. For instance they'll only feed you once a day. It might be at the same time every day but to my body clock it doesn't feel that way. Sometimes I think they skip a day or two. It's always a thin greasy chicken broth and one piece of bread and a cup of water. The cup and the bowl the broth comes in are made from dented tin instead of glass or ceramic that I might break to make a knife from. They don't want me to hurt myself. That's their job. They'll probably kill me when they're ready. I'm not sure about you because your crime might be different from mine. Not that I know what crime I'm here for.

This place is in a sad state. It looks diseased. You'll see when you're ready to come to the bars. In the cell to the left of yours big chunks of concrete have fallen from the ceiling. Water damage I guess. A pipe on an upper floor might have burst in the cold weather. And yes it gets even colder than this. It can get very hot as well. So hot you can't even draw in a breath the air is so thick. I've experienced changing seasons but I can't judge the passing of time from that because I think the heat comes on and off too. The furnace has to be as antiquated as the rest of this place. That is to say as much as I've seen of the rest of it. Which is only this bit of this hallway. The bars are rusted but they're still solid enough. You'll see the paint on the walls and ceiling is blistered and flakes of it have shed all over the floor. You can hear them crunching under the guards' boots when they come clomping to take me to the interrogation room. And just so you know they always blindfold me when they take me to and from the interrogation room. Which by the way is in as much a state of decrepitude as this hallway and our cells. Even the tin cup and bowl they bring my daily or maybe daily meal in are all dented and dinged as if a thousand prisoners before me drank and ate from them. I wonder if their tears dropped into the cup and bowl as they drank and ate like mine have done. Maybe I've drunk and eaten the residue of the tears of a thousand men. It surely feels like I have.

But you will come to love that dented little cup and that dented tin bowl. You will stare at the ghostly tease of your reflection in them and weep with self pity but also with a sickening gratitude. That's the genius of it. They can actually make you feel grateful. How much more broken can you be than to feel grateful for a bowl of greasy broth? It's the same gratitude I feel when they blindfold me to take me back to my cell. That means my daily beating has ended. I feel something like elation then. I feel elated that something has ended that should never have happened at all.

But who am I to say it shouldn't have happened when I don't even know what I might be guilty of?

You see the puddle on the floor between our cells? You

will if you just look up. Maybe you are looking up now but I can't see you crouched back there in the shadows. Anyway that puddle there gets much bigger sometimes before it dries up again though it never goes away entirely. It swells and recedes like it has its own tides. Anyway maybe water leaks from a pipe upstairs if there is an upstairs or maybe it's just the rain. Either way sometimes the puddle swells so much I can reach my hand through the bars and cup a little bit of water into my palm and bring it to my lips. Just a tiny tiny sip is all that's left after I scoop it up and bring it back through the bars but I'm grateful for it. It makes me feel a kind of triumph like I'm cheating them. Like I'm winning just a little. It's sad when you feel that such a thing is a triumph. Sad when you're grateful for a few drops of water stolen into the creases of your palm.

They play with my mind. It's like a beating to your soul. Twice they've brought me something other than chicken broth in my cherished tin bowl. My best friend tin bowl. Best friend before I knew you that is. Both times that other thing they brought me was a bowl of spaghetti. Yes! Can you believe it? A full bowl of spaghetti with tomato sauce and grated cheese sprinkled on top. Parmesan of course. And not only that but two plump juicy meatballs nestled in the noodles like eggs in a bird's nest.

The first time I thought it must be a guard's meal that was brought to me by mistake. Then I realized the guard only meant to torment me with it. He held it outside the bars but he didn't send it through the little hatch. Oh the steamy smell of the noodles! The acidic tang of the tomato sauce! I couldn't have been more moved to see the face of my own mother materialized before me. Couldn't have been more moved to see the face of God smiling at me with one hand extended to me and the other holding open the gate of a golden heaven. But my mother is long dead and I never believed in God. Which I think is probably the reason I'm here because the guard asked me something then that the interrogators always ask. He asked if I believed. I said yes! Yes of course I believe! I don't believe you he said. No no no I believe I said. I was salivating. I was sobbing so hard my shoulders shook.

I believe too he said. I believe I'm going to sit right here on the floor and eat this heavenly bowl of spaghetti. And he did. He did just that. Only a short space away from me on the other side of these rusted bars that guard sat there and chewed those fat meatballs and slurped up every strand of that pasta. But he left the last long strand dangling from his mouth. With one hand he took the other end and passed in between the bars. I reached for it but he scolded me around the end still in his mouth. I understood then and bent a little to take the free end of the strand in my own mouth. Then we each slurped our way to the middle of the strand. He kissed me through the bars and I could taste the tomato sauce and hamburger grease on his lips. I wanted to bite into those evil succulent lips. But instead when he stood up holding my precious empty bowl I fell onto my back and stared up at the ceiling and cried and cried. I cried for hours I think after he left. But I didn't just cry because I'd been denied that full bowl of spaghetti and those twin luscious meatballs. I also cried with gratitude because he had let me eat one half of one strand.

How I dreamed of spaghetti after that! One night if it was indeed nighttime I dreamed I was in a grove of spaghetti trees and beautiful naked women as plump as luscious meatballs were harvesting the long strands. Pulling the dangling tendrils out of the branches with one hand and adding them to big tin bowls they held against their fleshy hips with the other hand. I was naked too though much much thinner. Emaciated from near starvation. I had no bowl to collect the strands in so as I pulled each one down I stuffed it into my mouth. I ran through the aisles of the grove laughing and sobbing at the same time. Prancing like a madman pulling down fistfuls of noodles as

I passed. The women only looked over their shoulders at me and giggled. I crammed my mouth so full I couldn't open it again for fear that a big yarn ball of spaghetti would drop out and I'd be empty again. But I kept pulling down fistfuls of strands all the same until I finally fell down in the center of an aisle and rubbed those noodles all over my wasted ribs. I mushed the pasta against my skin as if to break it down to its original constituents of flour and water. But I felt an odd tickling across my skin that was not running beads of water. I lifted my head to look at my chest and saw dozens of small black insects scattering across my body. They were spaghetti weevils which in my dream I knew spoiled many a spaghetti crop. And when I realized the strands I had rubbed onto my chest had been infested with spaghetti weevils I then came to the realization that the noodles I had loaded into my mouth must be infested with weevils as well.

I sat up abruptly then and vomited up all the spaghetti I had ingested and stuffed in the pockets of my cheeks. Vomited myself empty again. And I woke up at that moment sitting up on my damp thin mattress and saw roaches drop off my chest onto my lap. I vomited then but it was only dry heaves.

That certainly wasn't the only nightmare their torture inspired though. In another dream I was standing on the roof of an office tower in a large city and other people stood with me or atop other skyscrapers. Blocking out the sun was a single huge thundercloud slowly drifting over the city. It was constantly streaming long bolts of lightning beneath it but it was odd that the lightning was also silhouetted darkly against the otherwise bright blue sky. And there was no sound of thunder either. Just the loud noise the crowds atop the buildings made. I didn't know if these were cries of fear or joy. I myself stood rooted in awed silence.

As the storm cloud floated nearer I could see the squirming bolts of lightning were actually curling around the tiny people congregated on the rooftops and pulling them up inside the churning dark cloud. They were not lightning bolts but long tendrils like those of a jellyfish. But they weren't even that! Because as the cloud came closer it no longer eclipsed the sun from my angle and I saw it for what it truly was. A monster. A God. A God formed from giant strands of spaghetti. Two eyes perched atop stalks like those of a crab scanned the massed people below. And no one was fleeing in terror as the dangling noodles wrapped around people and carried them up to stuff them into the depths of the spaghetti God. Into its body all convoluted like the folds of a human brain. No. These people wanted to be uplifted. They raised their arms to the God. It was a rapture.

Great drops of tomato sauce occasionally dripped down from its top side. I saw a drop hit a man on a nearby roof and its weight knocked him onto his back but he rubbed his hands across his chest and then licked them. Others around him dropped down beside him to rub their hands across him too. They also licked their palms as if drinking the God's holy blood.

Now the God hovered directly above the building I stood on and it was only me not raising my arms and crying out in ecstasy to the thing. I watched its tentacle noodles snatch up one person after another. The true believers.

The cold mindless eyes on their stalks shifted and I knew they gazed down directly at me. I couldn't run but neither could I be a liar and raise my arms to this monstrosity and accept it as my God. The creature looked straight down into my soul and could see this. And so it lashed out one whip-like arm at me. But the monster didn't pick me up and stuff me between those two testicle-like meatballs wedged into its front. Instead the tentacle flicked me as one might flick a bug with a finger. I was sent airborne. Up over the edge of the skyscraper's roof. And then of course I fell. Fell and fell toward the street so far below.

All the way down I screamed but I couldn't hear my own voice for all the voices that formed that chorus of adoration.

Again I woke with a start just as I was about to hit the pavement. In the gloomy corridor beyond the bars of my cell I saw eyes staring in at me. Cold mindless eyes on stalks above a seething body made of shadow. But the shadow shape faded and the eyes were the last to go. In only a second or two the image was gone and I was left to wonder if it had just been a lingering shred of the dream or if the thing outside had in fact been real and sent that nightmare into my head.

Maybe this was my true jailer. This scorned God whom I had rejected for his monstrous absurdity.

But what God isn't monstrous and absurd?

One of my dreams was suffered while I was unconscious on the floor of the interrogation room. Drops of blood ran down my face. But it wasn't blood. It was tomato sauce. I opened my eyes to find a less gigantic incarnation of that pasta abomination hovering just above me. Those lidless eyes on their stalks appeared to hold amusement somehow. Between the two meatballs one of the thick white noodles was extended and inserted into my gaping mouth. The God I rejected in my soul was forcing me to take its communion.

Do you know what communion wafers are made from? Flour and water.

But the noodle as it plumbed my soul gagged me and my mind cleared. It wasn't the spaghetti beast positioned above me but one of the interrogators. Not a noodle. Not two meatballs. His eyes were full of that same amusement however.

I told you they brought me spaghetti on two occasions. The first inspired these bad dreams so the second time I was wary. I expected the guard to sit down on the floor outside my cell and eat all the contents from the Holy Grail that was my dimpled tin bowl. It was the same guard after all. But instead he opened my food hatch and pushed the entire bowl in. I never had utensils when I received my soup. I just picked up the bowl and slurped it. I wasn't given utensils this time either but I couldn't have cared less. My hands were all the utensils I needed as I dug both of them into the pasta and brought it in two fistfuls to my mouth. I stuffed my cheeks just as in the dream of the spaghetti trees with tears of rapture running down my face.

But immediately I knew something was wrong. The slippery noodles squirmed of their own volition in my hands. In my mouth. And the one meatball I had also scooped into my mouth just tasted so wrong.

I looked down into my bowl again and saw what a thick covering of tomato sauce had masked before. It was not a bowl of spaghetti but a bowl filled with tangled writhing worms. And now I could tell that the remaining meatball in its nest of worms was shaped from human excrement.

The guard had started off down the hallway already. He didn't wait to see my expression. Didn't have to. I heard his laughter recede until he was gone.

I vomited up the worms and excrement. I stared down at the mess on the floor of my cell.

And then only a few minutes later I was stuffing earthworms into my mouth again. And I wept again but with gratitude this time as my stomach accepted this impromptu protein.

But I skipped the meatball.

Your own sobbing has increased I see. I understand. You sympathize with me but worse than that you realize now the treatment you yourself will have to endure. I truly wish that wasn't the case my friend. But at least now we'll no longer have to face our trials alone. Will we?

Hello? Hm.

Something occurs to me now. Maybe it's not fair of me but I have to say it. It's just that it seems so funny they'd give me company by putting another prisoner directly across from me.

I know you're crying and all and it sounds very sincere. But maybe you aren't who you seem. Maybe you're one of them. Huh? Maybe they think I'll spill some information that I never confess in my interrogations. Well if that's the deal I have to tell you I have nothing to confess because I don't know what it is they want me to confess to. How can I repent if I don't know my sins?

But if it's their God they want me to believe in then okay. Okay I believe in him. I've seen him so I believe. His presence was so strong in my dreams I'm sure there's more to him than only illusion. He's as real as any God except that he also happens to be made from flour and water in addition to illusion and delusion.

He's the Eucharist that eats you instead of you eating it. His followers are his communion wafers. Their tears of rapture are his water into wine.

I believe. You hear me? I believe.

Yeah I'm right aren't I? But maybe it's more than that. Maybe you're not just a spy.

I can barely bring myself to say it but maybe you're waiting for me to say it. You're him. The God himself. The same incarnation I saw peeking in through the bars at me when I woke from my dream. These bars are in effect your tentacles aren't they? You want to hold me in your hand and slowly squeeze me. Squeeze me in your spaghetti fingers. But haven't you squeezed everything out of me already? How long must this torture go on for?

Do you hear me? Do I have to shout even louder so the guards will come and beat me in my cell for a change instead of the interrogation room?

I believe in you! I believe you bastard! But I don't worship you! Squeeze me into tomato sauce between your giant fingers but I will never be your servant! I'm not just another of your mindless sheep! You think I'll let you eat me like those others?

I'll eat you instead! I'll suck down every last giant delicious strand of you! Who will be the God then? You want belief? Well you'd better believe me you fuck! Do you hear me? Huh?

Ohh. I'd better calm down. I really don't want them to come here. I've got to get a grip.

No more fake sobbing huh? All is nice and quiet. Sure. Why hold onto the charade anymore?

Hello?

My sweet lord? My tasty scrumptious parmesan-sprinkled lord?

Halloo!

Hm.

Okay. Okay. I can see you're not really there at all. Are you? No friend. No spy. No deity.

To tell you the truth it isn't the first time I thought I had company in that cell. It must be the way it makes my voice echo. It catches my voice over there like it's imprisoning another part of me. I shouldn't misinterpret my sobbing because I should know by now that I can cry and speak at the same time. Just like I'm doing now.

Oh! It's a good thing I quieted down. I hear the guard coming with my lunch. That is I hope it's lunch he's carrying and not his truncheon.

But there's something I hope even more than that.

I hope my revered tin bowl isn't full of spaghetti.

unwittingly, the italians excel at religious iconography once again

by Poncho Peligroso

a being of sufficient power to see and understand that all
time happens at once
    has the savvy to look before the time in which it existed
and think
    "there's something to be done about this"
    and wills itself into being

a being with the perception to see and understand
that the universe is a perfect two dimensional plane
and the strength to jump across it from point to point
can seemingly teleport anywhere in the universe at will
and so Nyarlathotep goes dancing across the fabric

a being which sees that waking life and dreams do not
need to be separate
    decides to bridge the gap with its womb
    and so Shub-Niggurath births nightmare monstrosities
unto Earth

from the creeping dark

in that dark
beyond the veil
a being cast out for questioning the authority of his mass-
murdering superior
Satan waits

at the center of creation there is a mad creator
a blind idiot
the voices and floods and storms of the old testament
the fool fools pray to, Azathoth the crawling chaos waits

in chains

endless curled pasta traps the idiot God
it has been this way for two thousand years now
spaghetti ended the time of earthly miracles
no more floods or plagues on a maniac's whim

the benevolent monster now does naught but regard
but we may thank him for freeing us

a being with the power to see all and the wisdom to let it
be
catches a small teapot as it drifts through space

BELIEVE WITHOUT EVIDENCE

by Len Kuntz

No one would eat anymore.

These were the dark days, everyone becoming so gaunt, gaunt itself becoming the new black.

We shuffled. Zombies could generate better foot speed than any of us. Our skins grew slack.

At certain junctures, the town echoed with bones banging against bones, clattering almost arthritic, without any sense of rhythm or percussion, but rather like a chimeless xylophone denoting imminent doom.

We were dying and we would do it together if that's what it took.

A little girl with corkscrew red hair came up to me and said, "You're a fucking nutjob." When I asked, "Excuse me?" and bent down, she spat on my face.

A boy that was the spitting image of Tiny Tim hobbled up to me and said, "I'm telling you, if you're wrong about this, then we've surely sprung out of a donkey's ass."

But I believed and so the others rather reluctantly followed suit. We all wanted it to be true. We wanted hope to be a word that meant something.

"How long must we wait?" they all asked on occasion.

I had no more answers than anyone. It could be years. It could be as short as minutes.

Most of us saw this self-imposed fast as a spiritual test of our faith. It felt good to care about something again. It had been so long since we'd sacrificed.

Still, some people had other ideas. Some wanted to throw a party to end all parties, make a calamitous racket, do it up old school-style, replete with kegs, funnelators, and vats of Spodieodie. "If He sees what a fun group we are, perhaps He'll want to join in," this group said.

Others thought the local yokel mayor or someone with political pull should drag out the klieg lights and nightly Swype text messages in the sky, communications of resolve but nothing too desperate.

Despite differences of opinions about strategy, we mostly all believed. We were willing to wait however long it took the carbo-loaded Messiah to return.

We took turns marking off days.

We became celibate and chaste if only because we'd lost our energy and sex seemed a cruel ruse, like well-written fiction.

We turned our last bits of energy toward Him, willing His homecoming.

Some said He lived in the shadows, all stringy and quietly breathing. Others said He showed up as a faint burn spot in their morning toast. Mad Hatters claimed His wrath was the reason for the world's plagues and famines. Many were quietly hoping He would return and decimate all the disgusting reality TV shows. Still, the poorest of the poor, the lepers and the feeble, prayed for His reappearance so as to make sense of their plight.

One Saturday night in May, a cousin from Calcutta was praying that someone would give him an answer as to whether he should continue in misery or take his own life. As he began screaming skyward, the atmosphere started convulsing. It was not the ground trembling, as in an earthquake, but instead the heavens. They vaulted and revolted. They roiled.

He called to tell me. "Cuz," he said, "are you awake?" There was a time zone difference, us being continents away. "You have to wake up and see! He is risen!"

I stumbled to my window and saw what my astonished cousin must also have been seeing. The sky was a whisk of cloud-swept canvas, entirely beige. I opened the door and breathed in the smell of steaming pasta.

And then it began to rain sphagetti.

Strips of Him fell from the heavens. Our manna. Giant hunks of noodles bounced off roofs, onto lawns, atop cars. Kids ran into the streets and bit right in, savage yet squealing. Parents applauded. It was a cacophony of cheering and foot stomping.

But then a neighbor pulled out a shotgun and started shooting. Soon fighter jets soared overhead, scarlet bullets blazing. Helicopters bombarded the air with infrared shells. Within minutes, the sky smoldered black soot and fireworks.

The Flying Spaghetti Monster appeared befuddled, stunned. His ropy blonde face had looked so serene and angelic moments earlier. Now it changed to purple wrath.

He stopped feeding us. He lassoed one jet after another, tossing them toward the ocean. An air-guided missile sliced through the barrage of flailing noodle arms and tore out a section of TFSM's lower abdomen, about the size of Delaware, and falling, the massive piece of pasta landed with a thunderous thud, crushing a few thousand spectators.

Sirens blared. Alarms. Heaven was at war, but only for that burst of time, because TFSM had had enough. He raised one giant noodle from his fist, flipping us all off, then flew away in a huff.

Jets chased him for a while, but none could match TFSM's supersonic speed. And besides, the army had accomplished its mission by scaring TFSM away. He wouldn't be back. Not in our lifetime.

People who witnessed the debacle on that day still trust in the pasta Messiah. But that was years and years ago, and they, like me, have gotten on in age. We'll die off soon, the way World War I vets have, yet we remain loyal.

When I tell my grandchildren TFSM stories, they make cracks about dementia. They pat me on the head. They give me a soft wink and shadow box the air around my ears. Rude little shits.

They can have their joking, the ignorant nitwits.

I see how the clouds resemble mounds of spaghetti. I get whiffs of freshly made noodles on windy days. When I look up at the heavens, I know he's there watching, waiting. It shouldn't be too much longer before he throws himself a good old Armageddon, wrings the necks of his enemies and drowns the unfaithful in oceans of marinara.

DARWIN'S REVENGE

by Bruce Taylor

Dr. Gruuper was, I would say, a curmudgeon. He rather looked like a fish in some weird way. Was it because he always wore gray slacks, white shirt, gray sports coat and with the big eyes, partially opened mouth and gray hair cut short—somehow, tanned skin not withstanding, I thought of him like a huge, well-fed guppy. I kept wondering if his legs hadn't somehow been grafted on him.

But that is, of course, where the similarities ended. As the assistant to the director of the museum, well, since the Director, Dr. Antonio Sepulveda was always running off to South America to examine some new Inca find in Chile or Peru or wherever and gone for extensively long times, Dr Gruuper actually was the *de facto* head of the museum.

For the sake of the ongoing investigation regarding our recent and most unusual find, much I cannot say, since I'm in charge of new exhibits and acquisitions (always a joy to draw crowds to the museum) and can only say what I saw. As for Dr. Gruuper, he still hasn't returned to the museum. (Probably for good reason.)

Anyway, not too long ago, when Intelligent Design was having yet another go at trying to get creationism in the schools, that's when the following took place.

I, being from Tacoma, Washington, where the Evolution Institute was headquartered (a keen source of embarrassment to me), resented what the Institute was doing, since it was clearly obvious that what was coming out of the Evolution Institute was nothing more than a means of "evolving" new ways of convincing the public and school districts that they possessed other motives, aside from getting creationism in the schools.. Their argument was so transparent: Really. Honestly. Darwin's Theory of Evolution was actually just a theory and other forms of thinking had to be examined about how life in its great complexity could possibly come to be. Therefore, there had to be a vast and Intelligent Agent at work for only such an amazing entity or some God-like (we're not saying we believe in a god, here) designer could possibly have the mental capacity to create and *blah blah, blah*—you get the picture. All the vast billions of years of evolution were totally inadequate to describe the current state of life on the planet and only the Great Intelligence of a Creative Genius could be the final answer.

This drove Dr. Gruuper absolutely insane. Every mention of the Evolution Institute made him nuts.

At the height of the controversy, when it was getting most heated in the media and the papers and the pundits on Faux News were saying stuff like, "—well maybe they have a point and maybe given how complex the universe is, maybe evolution can't explain it" and so forth and so on, and more than once, walking by Dr. Gruuper's office (actually fairly large but looked small because of the piles of books and papers stacked everywhere), I'd see him, reading the paper about the latest assault on Reason and he'd throw the paper down and say something like, "Jesus H. Christ why can't we be free of this stupidity? God Almighty, will this Intelligent Design shit *never* cease?"

Mind you, he didn't care if the door was open or closed; he'd get so upset if someone mentioned it that he'd vent anywhere—from the dinosaur exhibit to the great ape exhibit.

Once in a while after an explosive rant, he might see me and shake his head and say, "That the Age of Enlightenment is becoming the Age of Ignorance." Then he might go back to his office, sit, lean forward, elbows on desk and just rub his eyes with his palms.

Truly exasperated.

And you just have to wonder where such true and potent exasperation can take someone? Someone—like Dr. Gruuper who was truly exasperated. Who was also really well off, who had a reputation as a maverick, a scientific wunderkind, and a few patents in the field of genetics and—who was so pissed. So, so pissed. And I saw how it was getting to him when a light, wisp of an high school girl (with gold crosses for earrings) raised her hand after Dr. Gruuper explained in precise detail Darwin's Theory.

"Yes," he said, "question?"

She cleared her throat. "The Bible says that the earth is only 6,000 years old and since God is the agent of Intelligent Design—"

She stopped when Dr. Gruuper bowed his head a bit and rubbed his eyes.

Involuntarily, she stepped back.

Dr. Gruuper let out this incredible, long suffering sigh. "Even if there was a Supreme Being in charge of this all," Dr. Gruuper said to the girl who looked like she was just about ready to vanish into thin air and was probably, really sorry for bringing up that question. "Why can't evolution explain where we are now? Evolution has been acting on the species of this planet a lot longer than the theory of Intelligent Design, which is nothing more than creationism in disguise. Intelligent Design isn't about science, it's about religion. Just another way of getting science out of the picture so we can say 'God created it all.' Even if it were a god, who are *we* to fathom the mind of such an entity without ourselves becoming that god? It isn't the question of Intelligent Design—if anything; it's more like Unintelligible Design. We cannot know why the world is the way it is, but we know that it has evolved and that's what Darwin saw. Why does it have to be attributed to a creator, particularly a creator that looks an awful lot like a fundamentalist Christian concept of God?" (Later on he said, "It took everything I had not to go ballistic and tell her that Intelligent Design made as much sense as life created by a flying spaghetti monster." He grinned then shrugged. "Same thing.")

Some other things about Dr. Gruuper you should probably know—he came from the New Delhi branch of NovaGenetica, where he was a director of research ("Great job," he once said casually, "but they got a little antsy when I pushed them about honoring their mandate of daring new ideas to explore. They didn't seem to like mine." Shrug. Smile. "Sure paid me well to take a leave."). He took the job at the museum, where he thought he might be in a more public role about genetics and evolution, which were of immense fascination to him—"But I just can't accept the wanton ignorance of a public so desperate for answers that they're willing to abandon all sense and reason for an easy answer to the evolution of life."

So it didn't really come as too much of a surprise one day when, on my way to look over the work on a new exhibit dealing with animal intelligence, Dr. Gruuper waved to me from his office. "Mr. Jackson, may I see you for a minute?"

I stopped, surprised. Though we were certainly cordial and respectful to each other, he seldom asked me into his office.

Squeeeek. He leaned back in his chair, an old wooden swivel affair, put his hands behind his head. On the desk, the *Tacoma News Intelligencer* headlines, front page, lower right, "Intelligent Design Legal Challenge Enters Tenth Week."

He pointed to a serviceable strait back chair sans cushion and motioned me to pull it toward his desk. I did. And sat.

He stabbed his finger on the paper, "That there should even *be* an investigation!" he snarled. "It's like investigating the claim that the Earth is flat or that global warming is a hoax. Why do we spend the time and energy on such lunacy?"

I shrugged. "What's there to say? People like being stupid? People are afraid of thinking ?" I said, "I don't know."

"Well," he said, still fuming, "Well—I'm going." He stopped. Cleared his throat, "Something really should be done about this—this—" he gestured at the article, "—this—blatant disregard—" He stopped then, sighing, and looked about the paper-strewn desk. He rubbed his eyes with his palms and flopped his hands into his lap. "I've decided to take a little," he paused, "vacation. Maybe head out and help set up a little bio-tech firm somewhere where it's warm and tropical. Then again," he added, looking a bit mischievous, "maybe not. Never know." He sighed, sounding as if he thought he had made a good decision. Then he smiled. Right then he didn't look like a fish. Eyes bright, animated. "You're in charge for the next few weeks. Been cleared with Antonio. When he gets back in a week he'll be way too busy to do much around here. But at least you won't be on your own. Oh, yeah, your salary goes up thirty percent." He smiled sweetly. "Hope you don't mind."

Suddenly this looked like a really good deal. "OK," I said. I had been here long enough to know pretty much what went on and though this was more administrative than I wanted, a thirty percent raise wouldn't hurt.

We shook hands. For the next few days, he told me what was going on, what I needed to do, which media folks mattered, who was coming to town that I needed to pick up at the airport and help arrange a lecture, and that was that.

Then he was gone.

Weeks came. And went. Three months came—and went.

As did four months—then six months. Dr. Sepulveda assured me, until I pretty well memorized his spiel, that I *was doing a fine job*, and that *Dr. Gruuper would be coming back "before too long"* but until then, just—*continue on and, oh, by the way heading off to Colombia (or Peru or Ecuador) new discovery there, you'll be fine, you have my cell number and my email address and*—

—and I was in charge. Not what I had in mind. I had been getting occasional e-mails about what Dr. Gruuper was up to. Sort of. Leaving out a lot of details, but he was traveling and then—no e-mails for a while. Finally one came with a vague reference to heading off to Malaysia and "other places in the tropics." I asked in subsequent e-mails, after updating this and that about the museum, what he was doing and what his plans were, but he never responded to those questions. He did ask occasionally, how the investigation was going in regard to the Evolution Institute. I'd tell him the latest news. Rumor was that deep pockets were funding the Institute. It seemed like this could go on for a time. A *long* time. The controversy over the Institute, as well as the entire city of Tacoma, had become the subject of withering ridicule with embarrassing skits, take-offs, and commentaries on the late night talk shows (the most recent one, on the *Daily Night Report*, with Stephen Stewart, a sandy-haired bear of a guy, with a huge following and on one particular night in question, he came out on stage, and, slapping his hands together and holding them in front of him, said, "Hey, how about that new Scopes Trial in Tacoma, Washington? They call it the City of Destiny. Wow! Oh, boy! Destined to be remembered as the location of the Evolution Institute—way to go Ta-COH-ma—the City of De-Evolution!"). Dr. Gruuper sent me an email not long after suggesting that, for the sake of my pride, it might be smart of me to change my place of birth on all legal documents. He put a little, yellow smile icon behind that statement.

It was probably a week after Stephen Stewart made that

comment that, in our weekly delivery of items for the museum, I got a call from receiving; the driver had a special delivery for New Acquisitions. Would I okay it? "Sure," I said, "Trillium will deal with it." A few minutes later, I got a call from (Sandee) Trillium. She was one of Gruuper's cousins and had been hired on around the same time as him. There was a clear hesitancy in her voice. "Hi, Sandee here. Um—I think you'd better get down here."

I looked at my schedule. Wow. No way. "Hey, Sandee, Can we make it later? I have an awful—"

"—uh—yeah—but—uh—you'd better get down here." *Click.*

Irritated, I nonetheless hustled down to Acquisitions and saw her slim, short form in her usual jeans and blue shirt; her dark hair pulled back as always and her brown eyes looking— worried. Standing next to her, looking like a giant, her assistant, Jack Metcalf with usual tee-shirt on, glasses down his nose a bit and his usually boyish face and ready smile—well, he was looking a bit off.

"Um," Sandee began, pointing to an animal carrying cage on the counter where we checked stuff in. "This came just now. No way to return it."

I looked at the carrying cage—tan, horizontal bars across the door and plastered with stickers: LIVE ANIMAL, CAUTION, and a fancy sticker, red and white in the shape of a five-pointed star: N.C.R.I. and below it, *New Caledonia Research Institute, Noumea, Gran Terre Island, New Caledonia.*

"We tried to Google the place," said Jack, "but nothing comes up. Near as we can tell—uh—we wonder if it's maybe like a post office box or something," he trailed off and lifted his hands in a "beats me" gesture.

There was an opened, thick padded, shipping envelope on the side. And something in the cage kept going (softly) "snuffle-wuffle—ah-whooo. Ah-whoo."

"I opened the envelope," said Sandee. She handed me a cassette tape and several pictures. I stared at the pictures—shots of red—*somethings*—about the size of basketballs and almost as round, on a rocky beach and from the shots, even away from the beach—looked like there was mighty sparse vegetation. Initial thought was that it was a volcanic landscape; a hot and bleak place. But, though the shots looked like they were taken from a distance, clearly the landscape was lavish with these—whatever's.

I looked back to the carrying cage, and through the bars in front, a bright orange bill, like a duck, poked out. I slowly put my finger up to it. What ever it was gently nibbled at my forefinger. I shrugged. "Well? Looks harmless enough." I opened the door to the cage. Pause. Then slowly—something waddled out. Something red, round and—what came to my mind was the scene out of *Forbidden Planet* where Doc had made a plaster cast of the footprint of the, later to be known, Monster from the Id, and Doc is saying, "This thing runs counter to every known law of adaptive evolution. This is anywhere in the galaxy a nightmare."

But it wasn't *exactly* a nightmare. Running counter to all laws of adaptive evolution, it most certainly did—but—more out of nature having fun—experimenting? Maybe nature a little bit—drunk? Or—high on something? We stared at it. Body clearly not oriented for flying; rudimentary wings. Long, red feathers, but feathers you would find on birds in cold climates—hardly a warm one. Legs that bent forwards, *not* backwards for what evolution-ary purpose we could not possibly imagine. Feet that you find for birds in a jungle or wet climate, but not adapted for the kind of landscape we saw. A long bill and broad head, and,with the bluest, most sincere and beautiful eyes—facing forward, like an owl.

It looked up at us as if examining each one of us carefully with an absolutely unnerving intelligence. Then, softly, "Ah-whoooo?"

Sandee just shook her head. "What on Earth *is* it?"

I looked at the cassette in my hand. "Tape recorder someone?"

Jack produced one. "Took some looking." He plopped it down on top of the cage; it was an older, Panasonic, well-used, serviceable, but I had to wonder why a tape instead of a CD or a DVD or something to do with computers—I shrugged. No idea. But I put the cassette in, hit play. Music—The Beatles, "Help!"

The what-ever-it-was, just looked around. "Ah-whooo."

Simon and Garfunkle, "At the Zoo"

Nothing. Just calmly looking about.

"Mandy," by Barry Manilow.

The creature immediately perked up, began to stomp its feet, then moving and "Ah-whoo-ing" and moving in time to the music. The piece cut off, then, The Rolling Stones, "Let's Spend the Night Together."

The creature just ruffled its feathers and appeared somehow vexed, as if it had a headache.

Then the theme music to "The Lawrence Welk Show." Again. the creature became alive and this time, with voice sounding like a kazoo, hummed along with the music.

This was followed by a (clearly altered) voice on the tape (I found myself thinking there was something very familiar about that voice, altered as it was, but I just couldn't be sure) and we heard poetry, identified as from a book, *Listen to the Warm* by Rod McKuen. After several words, the creature abruptly stiffened and appeared to have a seizure. The voice stopped. The animal recovered, instantly, looking around again as if nothing happened. The voice resumed, and it was "The Love Song of J. Alfred Prufrock" by T.S. Eliot and by the time the poem got to, "I grow old/I grow old/I wear the bottoms/of my trousers rolled—" there exuded from our little friend a great sadness; its blue eyes welled up with—tears? We stared. *Tears?* Then it settled down, laying its head on top of a book Jack had been reading on his breaks, *The Best Short Stories of H. G. Wells*, and exhaled a long, sad and forlorn, "Ah-whaaa-whoooo."

"Something else," Sandee said, handing me a plastic wrapped item. A Hostess Twinkie. I began to open the package and at the sound of tearing plastic, the creature came out of its torpor instantly, "Ah-whoop! Ah-whoop! Ah-whoop!" and leaped to snatch the Twinkie from my hand, devouring it in a gulp. A bizarre thought came to my head. *Could a bird exposed to Twinkies…mutate?*

The creature made another gulp and looked up at me in eager anticipation.

We all looked to each other. The same thought between us all—*Of what possible adaptive advantages—why—even the wrapper.*

Then the thought occurred to me, what Dr. Gruuper had said, "Unintelligible design—not intelligent design, not unintelligent design—" but more like—then I got it—like—*cunning design, clever design.* Something was making sense—and then I had a lightning flash of insight and that "AHA" moment and I suddenly had a real strong hunch what this was about and I laughed and announced, "OK. Boy! Wouldn't it be a shame if the press got a hold of this—and *right* during this big deal on Intelligent Design? But," and I held up my finger in a stern warning, "if this gets leaked to the press, I guarantee dire consequences for the culprits—they will have to suffer pizza and beer."

"Oh, no!" Sandee clapped her hands in mock horror. "How awful!"

Jack had his boyish grin back and even more so. "Oh, hey! Not to worry! we'll make sure that does *not* happen! By the way, I want Swiss cheese and pepperoni."

Two hours later, the press was all over the place. By that time, we were pretty buzzed from being beered and pizza-ed to the max and had named our little friend "Niwrad" in honor of Darwin who couldn't know that sometimes evolution might be impacted by forces that he simply could not recognize or know about though, in the purest sense, something told me that this creature probably wasn't evolution at work, per se, but as I thought more about all this, in a world where toxins in the environment are resulting in two headed frogs, sexually mature eight-year-old girls, and all the other strangeness of evolution now going amuck and anything but intelligent design playing a part in such biological horrors, and more like maladaptive design going on—well, what's a little more tampering with nature by nature or—or—*maybe*, I smiled, *someone?*

Anyway, the press went nuts.

"Retro-Darwin!" was the banner headline in the *Seattle News Tribune*. "Unintelligent Design?" as the headline in a New York paper, and others headlines were equally funny and strange. The interviews we had were great as now Niwrad was all over the media, YouTube, as it (still wasn't sure of the sex) waltzed and kazooed to Lawrence Welk (revived interest in the show) and sales of Barry Manilow went through the roof. And in all this, in all this, maybe a week or so later, a little noticed head-line on page 6 of the *Seattle News Tribune*: "Evolution Institute Withdraws Suit: Agrees to pay all legal costs." And a few days after that, another little headline, in the "Local Events" section that occupied the right half of the comic page, and (coinciden-tally?) right beside the "B.C." comic strip: "Evolution Institute Closes Due to Lack of Funds."

And somehow, someway, though I can't prove a thing, nor would I, I fancy I dreamed one night that I saw Dr. Gruuper laughing, holding a paper ("Patent Grant" stamped on the top) and standing on a rocky, blocky beach, alive with Niwrads, all humming, hopping and bopping to the music of Barry Manilow.

ALL CHILDREN GO TO HELL

by Kevin L. Donihe

Bored and lonely, Robbie moped in his pale blue room. He'd broken a vase out of spite, and his parents had banished him, indefinitely, to his train-shaped bed. There was to be no TV, no snacks. He was permitted to read, but books didn't interest him. Hours later, he still sat on his mattress, fists propped against his chin, staring at his chest of drawers and thinking about the world outside.

Suddenly, his window flew open. Through it glided a monster of densely coiled pasta, chunky tomato sauce atop its head. Lips formed a doughy smile as the monster regarded Robbie with oversized meatball eyes. Standing before him, it seemed larger than the room.

The boy was confused, but didn't feel threatened. The monster looked funny and smelled of Spaghetti Os, his favorite food since kindergarten. Nothing so silly and delicious would hurt him, he figured.

After nearly a minute of silence, Robbie asked, "What are you?"

A sonorous voice replied, "I am the Flying Spaghetti Monster."

He then asked what it wanted.

"To show my best friend a magic trick." It paused, cocked its head. "Are you my best friend, Robbie?"

Words failed the boy, so the spaghetti monster said, "I know everything. Become my best friend, and I'll prove it."

But Robbie already had a best friend. His name was Ben, and together they played ball, caught and killed bugs, and built forts of pillows and snow. It seemed wrong to abandon Ben for a creature he'd just met—but he wanted, more than anything, to see magic on an otherwise gray and boring day.

"Yes," Robbie said, finally. "You're my best friend."

"So rub me. See what I can do."

Robbie sat there, staring. What it had said reminded him of the things sweaty, balding men told little boys in weird videos his parents had made him watch. Again, he thought of Spaghetti Os, but still trembled as he left the mattress and reached for the monster.

Beneath his fingers, individual pasta strands felt electric and throbbed like veins. When he rubbed, the strands became motile, twisting around and spiraling into one another as the monster grew. Soon, it was bigger than the house—the Earth—yet expansion continued. Faced with noodles longer than river systems, the boy stopped rubbing.

"Now enter me," the monster said. "It's warm and cozy inside."

Robbie thought food should enter people, but then recalled gingerbread houses where storybook characters lived. Perhaps this was a similar arrangement, and who else in his school could say they'd been inside a spaghetti monster?

"Will I see guts?" he asked, sheepishly.

It laughed as belly strands parted like a curtain. Climbing inside, Robbie found a cavernous hall of white. It was indeed warm and cozy, no guts to be seen. Ahead of him, runners of spaghetti stretched out, knitting together to form a crude hammock. Robbie first sat in it, but his eyelids grew heavy, and he decided to rest.

His mind began to wander, so much so that Robbie forgot he had another home. On occasions, he saw himself outside the monster, but nothing beyond it seemed real. Dinnertime with parents was a gray blur with gray people with fading faces. Whenever they spoke, they said nothing of interest. School was more of the same. Other times, a different, younger voice would call to him, ask him to come out and play, but Robbie couldn't give it a name.

"You are ready," the monster said. "Now close your eyes."

Robbie did, and images snaked out from behind his lids, forming scenes. He saw himself bow before a litany of golden idols, men on trees, crosses, and a massive black cube. He saw himself burn incense and lie prostrate on prayer mats, then confess his sins to dark men in dark rooms and count beads in a rosary, over and over until his fingers bled. Then he clutched a knife—long, curved and glistening. Lifting it high, he let sunlight play on the blade before plunging it into the guts of a tied-down, struggling bull. A moment later, he slid a different knife across the throat of a GI Joe.

A thousand such scenes converged in his mind, meshing into a shaft of blinding white light. Bathed in it, Robbie could no longer think, no longer feel. He'd become all things at once.

No time and forever passed. Dimming, the light separated into component parts, returning the boy to consciousness as idols, prayer cloths, knives and beads were absorbed into the monster to become pasta again.

Suddenly, a booming voice: "You must leave me now."

"But I just got here," Robbie said, disappointed. "Can I stay longer?"

"No one can remain inside me forever, but don't be glum. I have another trick to show you."

Robbie perked at the promise. The first had been better than anything on TV, so he could only imagine how much greater a second trick might be.

Strands parted for him. He saw light, got up and stepped toward it, into a world where his room had become a soggy, decaying ruin. Windows had shattered. The ceiling sagged as brown-green mold grew wild on the carpet. Paper had dried, turned black and peeled from the wall. It littered the floor like dirty snow.

Robbie considered calling down for his parents, but knew they weren't there. Though the place was nothing if not vacant, it didn't concern him; his best friend had a new trick to show.

"Do it! Do it!" Robbie said, impatiently, and was surprised by the depth of his voice.

"I will, if you'll do one last thing for me." The strands of the monster's lips formed another, wider smile. "Make me your *only* friend."

Robbie opened his mouth, but closed it quickly. Perhaps it was best to have friends not made of pasta, sauce and bulbous mounds of meat, friends who didn't want him all to themselves. He thought hard, recalled a forgotten name, and felt a sudden twinge of regret.

"But Ben—"

"Ben has been gone for a while now," the monster said. "He's in a better place."

"He is?"

"You could go out and make new friends, of course—but why bother? I'm already here, aren't I?"

Robbie nodded.

"So do as I ask, and I'll show you the trick."

The offer was too tempting to refuse. "You're my only friend," Robbie said, and meant it.

The monster beaconed. "Then step up; rub me again."

Robbie obeyed, and the walls of his house collapsed and

turned to dust. Rotting beneath him, floorboards buckled before giving way. But he didn't fall into the basement. His one and only friend supported him even as it performed the same trick in reverse, becoming smaller than Robbie, then smaller than an infant. In seconds, the monster fit neatly in the boy's cupped palm.

Strands no longer pulsed; sheer electricity felt like mere static. Robbie rubbed with a single finger now, rubbed until the monster resembled an ant. Then he stopped, fearful that he might crush such a tiny and seemingly delicate thing.

"Don't worry, Robbie," it soothed in a still, small voice. "Nothing can harm or take from me. My essence is eternal."

Robbie didn't know all the words, but understood the gist, so he continued until it seemed that he held only air. The trick, he realized, had actually been a disappearing act.

"That was great!" he said. "Now show me another!"

From the emptiness in his palm, there came no reply.

"Are you there?" he continued.

Silence deepened, swallowing background noise. He glanced around, but saw that direction itself had failed him. There was no longer up or down, left or right. He had only his body and a void as eternal as the monster had once seemed. Immediately, he felt lost and alone, trapped and deceived. Dread took hold, then panic and all-consuming horror. Aimlessly, he flailed.

But in time-that-was-no-time, even terror died. Left with his thoughts, he studied the dark hairs and dry cracks of his withered hands. He wondered if his monster had been wrong, if he'd crushed it, if it was dead, or if it had even existed at all. Vision fading, he yearned for all the things he'd left behind, just for the promise of a little magic on a dull, boring day.

"Mom? Dad? Ben?" he called, voice breaking, but they were nothing.

And, in an instant, Robbie was nothing, too.

GRUMPY OLD GODS

by David W. Barbee

A dozen black flies buzzed out of the mighty Cthulhu's mouth. He yawned, and the god-beast of all terror and madness climbed out of bed, his fat gooey tentacles unsticking themselves from the slimy sheets.

Loud music blasted from the alarm clock as he pulled some clothes over his plump, squishy body. Today he picked his maroon sweat suit with the embroidered stegosauruses frolicking across the tummy. His tentacles poked out here and there, and his long squirmy beard flowed down over his chest.

Cthulhu smashed the alarm clock to bits and waddled out of his bedroom. He passed several framed photos in the hallway, pictures of him and his college buddies. They were posed at parties, dances, or graduation, all of them laughing and smiling.

Ah, college. Days of wild youthful abandon, before time even existed and when the universe had yet to be born. Before he'd had to move to this fucking suburb.

The suburb was home to all of the mythical gods and titans from across the cosmos. It was lined with neat little houses, each with a picket fence and concrete driveway. A deity lived in each house, which was his own universe unto itself, filled with billions of life forms to tend to.

It had been created back at the beginning of time by gods unknown. As mortal life forms worshipped an ever growing and diverse range of deities, the divine beings required a system of organization. They needed a place where each could have their own equally sized realm to rule over as they saw fit. So they built a suburb to house them all, and for the most part it was a success. Holy wars between feuding gods declined and there was peace.

But Cthulhu thought it was stupid. He so hated being organized. He thought the idea of phenomenally powerful beings sitting in these tiny little squares was patently absurd.

So he stayed inside and kept to himself. He didn't want to talk to others. The idea of it sickened him. Even his friends, the other Old Ones from the college days, weren't really friends at all. Bokrug was an arrogant jerk. Rhogog was pathetic and needy. And even Nyarlathotep fancied himself some sort of intellectual when even Cthulhu could tell he was full of shit. They were merely a series of acquaintances he'd stumbled upon, not people he actually liked or enjoyed. He didn't like or enjoy *anyone*.

As Cthulhu shuffled into his kitchen, the kittens were there to greet him, crowding the counters and awaiting their breakfast. They were scraggly little beasts with dingy fur and little flames pouring from their empty eye sockets. Several of the kittens crowded near Cthulhu and rubbed their faces against his legs. They burned bits of his sweatpants, but wet tentacles snaked out to extinguish the flames.

Some of the kittens had captured tiny humans, the little corpses impaled in their teeth. Try as he might, Cthulhu could never keep the pests from getting inside the house. There was always a nest of humans somewhere in the walls, but the kittens were usually able to hunt them down.

The kitchen was a cesspool of grout and mildew. Ancient dishes overflowed from the sink, and the bulky fridge contained scores of savage bacteria. Cthulhu reached up to a high cupboard and retrieved an old bag of kitty chow. He turned and emptied the bag across the slimy linoleum floor and the kittens pounced onto the food. The recipe for the chow was of Cthulhu's own making, made from puréed humans and squid brains. The kittens loved it.

He exited the kitchen for the living room, then plopped down on his duct-taped recliner and switched on his eighty-nine inch TV. The suburb provided cable to every house, but there were only five channels and Jesus Christ was always on four of them. Lucifer was on the fifth. The Great Satan was kind enough to broadcast twenty-four hour programming from his house, offering the best in hellish porn and talk shows that'd make you stab your eyes out with your own thumbs.

Cthulhu watched a few hours of hellporn, which brought him a sort of placid boredom.

Then it happened.

The noise was back again.

Cthulhu heard the warble at least once a day. It was soft and gentle yet strong enough to penetrate the walls of his house, and every day it drove him into a raging insanity.

He roared and pulled himself off the recliner. "Not again!"

Normally Cthulhu wouldn't bother to leave his house, but today he was particularly irritable. He stomped to the front door and threw it open.

Sunlight blasted Cthulhu's face and he was met by his front yard, walled in by the picket fence. It was an overgrown garden of flowering squid plants with wavy tentacle bushes. Like every other home in the suburb, Cthulhu's front yard was his cosmic domain, though he didn't tend to it as the other gods did. So what if Muhammad, Odin, and Zenu all kept better yards than him. He didn't care. None of it was worth the time or effort. Those who believed otherwise were both meaningless and stupid.

Hunks of crabgrass crept about Cthulhu's yard, snapping their pincers maniacally. Fat garden slugs hovered around on fluttering bat wings. Even the snails and shrubs had a demonic bent to them. And deep in the wild brush were the tiny humans, who were Cthulhu's devout worshippers.

They lived in cracked seashell homes and wore ragged loincloths made from their own hair. None of them had teeth and they spoke in a language of babbling rambles. Every other creature in the yard was the humans' predator. They were terrorized and slaughtered every day, which had driven them beyond insanity. And yet their entire miniature civilization was dedicated to the worship of Cthulhu, the mighty master of madness and oblivion.

Cthulhu hated the bastards.

The warbling noise went on and on. Across the picket fence, standing outside the house next door to Cthulhu, was the source of the goddamnable warbling.

The Spaghetti Monster.

Cthulhu hated his neighbor above all other gods. The Spaghetti Monster was a bigger bore than Buddha and more irritating than Joseph Smith. Cthulhu's hatred for this god was deeper than the deepest, blackest abyss. To the naked eye, the Monster appeared delightful and harmless, a tangled pile of pasta with meatball eyes and a noodly mouth that quivered and waved as he sang his warbly song. It was a pleasant song that he sang every day while tending his garden.

The grass of the Monster's yard was made from the same spaghetti as his flesh, with hedges that were dense hunks of lasagna. There were flowering plants of fettuccini, ravioli, rigatoni, and couscous. There were garden rocks made of meatballs, and bushes of breadsticks sprouted here and there. The Spaghetti Monster moseyed around, pouring thick red sauce from a watering can and singing.

Roaming across the noodles were tiny pirate ships full of millions of miniscule humans. They sailed across the lawn singing joyful pirate songs, pleasant and content just like their holy Spaghetti Monster. The Monster happily warbled to the millions of worshippers living in his yard as if they weren't vermin.

It was beautiful and serene, and Cthulhu threw up at the sight of it all. His vomit, a sea of radioactive swamp sludge, flooded across his yard and drowned most of his humans.

He hurried back into his house before anyone could see him. Things like that were why Cthulhu never left his house. He wrung out his tentacle beard, which was soaked with puke. He plopped back down onto his recliner and thought about what he'd just seen.

The Spaghetti Monster was so happy, and Cthulhu hated that. It figured that he would get stuck next door to the Spaghetti Monster instead of Krishna or Ganesh. Those guys knew how to party. They could be counted on to destroy shit here and there between philosophical ramblings. Not that Cthulhu liked those guys, but at least they were interesting.

The Spaghetti Monster, on the other hand, was boring. This, of course, was a direct sign that the Spaghetti Monster was an idiot.

Everyone was his friend.

He had no vices or enemies, which meant that he had no personality.

Nothing ever offended him because he didn't stand for anything.

Nothing outraged him because he was stupid.

To be peaceful and popular was just another way of being a complete fucking douchebag. In short, fuck the Spaghetti Monster. Right up his noodly asshole.

Then something occurred to Cthulhu. This was a problem that could be solved. He could rebel against the conformity of the suburb, the forced diversity, the iron fist that made neighbors of them all. These houses were prisons, and someone had to shake things up.

He had to kill the Spaghetti Monster.

Cthulhu wondered why no one had thought of it before. It

was revenge, really, and half the gods in the suburbs were vocal proponents of good old-fashioned revenge. Hell, Yahweh practically invented it.

He hurried to the kitchen, gingerly stepping through the army of kittens still slurping kitty chow off the floor. The kittens looked up as Cthulhu passed and instinctively knew his intentions. The little flames in their eye sockets burst into bigger fires that whipped and raged. They sang ancient epic chants in echoing voices.

Cthulhu opened his cupboards and drawers, shuffling things around until he found where he'd hidden his slaying knife. He pulled it from a cabinet, dislodging cockroaches and salamanders from the junk. The knife was twelve feet long, and Cthulhu gripped the handle with both hands. He couldn't remember the last time he'd been on an old-fashioned slaying.

Soon his flabby arms grew tired just holding the giant weapon. The blade sank to the floor with a clank and the kittens scattered. Cthulhu dragged it through his house, thinking of all the ways he'd make the Spaghetti Monster pay. His mind was filled with all the unspeakable wrath he would soon set down on that noodly bastard's head.

Cthulhu hobbled over to the front door. He dragged the slaying knife outside and across his puke-flooded front yard. He squished little monsters and worshippers under his tentacled feet, and the giant blade dug a rut behind him as he trudged toward the Monster's house. He walked through the picket fence, shredding it under his terrible march.

He approached a nice square window on the side of the house. It was slightly open, letting a breeze flow through the home. Cthulhu squeezed his spongy tentacled flesh through the slit, but the slaying knife got caught in the windowsill. Without a backwards glance he yanked the weapon through, shattering the window and most of the wall around it. He continued through the house, still dragging the knife behind him.

He took in the interior, which was just as neat and organized as the garden outside. The rooms were decorated like an Italian restaurant with a pirate theme. There were red-and-white checkered curtains, ship wheels, anchors, Jolly Rogers, and display cases full of cutlasses and flintlocks. There were framed photos of the Spaghetti Monster posing happily with brilliant scientists, artists, and thinkers, including the King of the Pirates, Charles Darwin.

It was gimmicky and cluttered, neat and organized.

Sickening.

Cthulhu continued on and found the Spaghetti Monster in the kitchen.

The Monster stood at the stove, stirring the contents of a steaming pot with a wooden spoon. His other hand scooped big clumps of noodles from his body, dropping them into the pot. He was holding a big clump of himself when Cthulhu came into the kitchen and let out a ferocious roar.

The Spaghetti Monster turned and warbled a happy hello.

It was the same stupid warbling, but now that Cthulhu was so close he began to hear it as actual words. The Spaghetti Monster was asking him to have a seat at the kitchen table. He said the noodles would be ready soon.

Cthulhu growled at the Monster. "I'm not here for your food," he said. "I've come to slay you."

The Spaghetti Monster warbled again.

"*Why* doesn't matter," Cthulhu said. "Don't you get it? I don't care. I can do what I want. I have given a name to my pain and that name is Spaghetti Monster!"

Another warble from the Spaghetti Monster.

"Well I guess that makes me fucking crazy!" Cthulhu roared. "I'm the god-beast of all terror and madness, stupid!"

The Spaghetti Monster said something else.

"No, I don't expect anything to change. But at least it'll end the tedium of living in this fucking suburb. Living here sucks, and the only thing worse is that they put me next door to *you*."

The Spaghetti Monster said nothing. He nodded his noodly

head at Cthulhu and walked away from the stove. He crossed the kitchen to the table and sat down in one of the chairs, leaving his back to Cthulhu. He waited.

"What? You're sacrificing yourself to me? You think that makes you noble or something? You're no different than the others. In fact, you're even worse. You're just a pile of spaghetti. You new gods, you don't understand how it used to be in prehistoric times. To be a god you had to be bigger than the sky. Now all you've gotta do is have a few morons click you on the internet. You don't even eat any of them."

A single tear formed in Cthulhu's beady black eye as he raised the slaying knife high over his head. He brought the giant blade down onto the Spaghetti Monster, slicing his soft noodly body in twain.

The slaying knife shattered the chair and embedded itself in the kitchen floor below. Cthulhu jerked it free and looked down at the Spaghetti Monster's dead body. The remains of the Monster sank to the floor in two noodly heaps. Thick tomato sauce and oblong meatballs leaked from the wounds.

Then something changed.

Cthulhu watched in horror as the noodles and sauce and meatballs began to swirl around and mix together. The two lumps on either side of the broken chair pulsed and throbbed and began to take new shapes.

They became two Spaghetti Monsters, and both turned to look at Cthulhu.

"No!" Cthulhu cried. Surely there was a way to destroy the Monster. Cthulhu roared and attacked again. He sliced both of them through their waists with the slaying knife, but that only made the two Spaghetti Monsters into four.

The four noodly beings began to warble amongst themselves, but Cthulhu could no longer understand the language. He was far too furious.

He screamed and attacked again. He went on chopping the Spaghetti Monsters for the rest of the day, but splitting the noodled bodies only caused them to multiply like cells. Cthulhu roared and raged as the Spaghetti Monsters multiplied, their warbling voices becoming as loud as thunder. Soon the slaying knife became dull and Cthulhu's arms went limp. He collapsed to the kitchen floor in exhaustion, surrounded by bumbling Spaghetti Monsters. They filled the entire house now, milling about and constantly warbling to one another.

Cthulhu puked again, this time in utter misery. The Spaghetti Monsters took no notice. They stepped through the putrid green sludge and started whipping up a feast of noodles, happily warbling away.

ABOUT THE EDITOR

Cameron Pierce is the author of six books, including *The Pickled Apocalypse of Pancake Island, Lost in Cat Brain Land,* and *Cthulhu Comes to the Vampire Kingdom.* As an editor for Lazy Fascist and Fantastic Planet Press, he has published books by such diverse writers as *New York Times* bestseller Piers Anthony, outsider indie sensation Sam Pink, and World Fantasy Award-winning artist Alan M. Clark. He lives in Portland, Oregon.

ABOUT THE AUTHORS

Kirsten Alene is the author of *Love in the Time of Dinosaurs*, published by the Eraserhead Press New Bizarro Author Series. Her work has appeared in *The Magazine of Bizarro Fiction*, *Christmas on Crack*, *Bust Down the Door and Eat All the Chickens*, *Nouns of Assemblage*, *New Dead Families*, *The Battered Suitcase*, and *Rivets*. She is also the fiction editor for Bizarro Central.

David W. Barbee is the author of *A Town Called Suckhole* and *Carnageland*. His work has appeared in Unicorn Knife Fight and *Technicolor Tentacles*. He loves peanut butter and hates cheese.

Kate Bernheimer has published novels, stories, children's books, creative nonfiction, and essays on fairy tales, and has edited three influential fairy tale anthologies, including *My Mother She Killed Me, My Father He Ate Me: Forty New Fairy Tales*.

Her most recent book is *Horse, Flower, Bird*. Published by Coffee House Press, it includes illustrations by Rikki Ducornet. Her children's book, *The Girl in the Castle Inside the Museum* (Random House/Schwartz & Wade Books), was named one of the Best Books of 2008 by Publishers Weekly. She has published fiction and literary nonfiction in such journals as *Tin House*, *Western Humanities Review*, *Poetry International*, and *The Massachusetts Review*.

In 2005, she founded, and currently remains editor of, *Fairy Tale Review*, the leading literary journal dedicated to fairy tales as a contemporary art form.

Adam Bolivar is a puppeteer who lives in Portland, Oregon.

S.G. Browne graduated from the University of the Pacific in Stockton, CA, and worked for several years in Hollywood doing post-production for the Disney Studios. His debut novel, *Breathers*, was optioned for film by Fox Searchlight Pictures, while the Washington Post called his second book, *Fated*, "A terrific comic novel." His writing is inspired by his love of dark comedy, social satire, and the supernatural. His third novel, *Lucky Bastard*, is due out in April 2012. You can visit him at www.sgbrowne.com.

Edmund Colell lives in Arizona. His stories have been published in the anthologies *Christmas on Crack* and *Technicolor Tentacles* as well as online at Bizarro Central and Verbicide.

Kevin L. Donihe is the Wonderland Book Award-winning author of *House of Houses, Night of the Assholes, Washer Mouth: The Man Who Was a Washing Machine, The Greatest Fucking Moment in Sports*, and other books. He is also the editor of *Walrus Tales*, the first ever walrus-themed fiction anthology.

Cody Goodfellow is the Wonderland Book Award-winning author of *Silent Weapons for Quiet Wars, Perfect Union*, and three books written with John Skipp, *Spore, Jake's Wake,* and *The Day Before*, along with many other works of tantalogical terror. His fiction has appeared in *Cemetery Dance, Black Static, Dark Discoveries, The Magazine of Bizarro Fiction, Flurb*, and many other publications.

Jess Gulbranson is the author of *10 A BOOT STOMPING 20 A HUMAN FACE 30 GOTO 10*. He lives in Portland, Oregon.

Mykle Hansen is the Wonderland Book Award-winning author of *Hooray for Death, Help! A Bear is Eating Me, The*

Cannibal's Guide to Ethical Living, *Eyeheart Everything*, and *The Rampaging Fuckers of Everything on the Crazy Shitting Planet of the Vomit Atmosphere*. A jack of all trades since birth, Mykle lives in Portland, Oregon.

Kirk Jones is the author of *Uncle Sam's Carnival of Copulating Inanimals*, published by the Eraserhead Press New Bizarro Author Series. His work has appeared or is forthcoming in *The New Flesh: Episode I*, *Technicolor Tentacles*, *A Hacked-Up Holiday Massacre*, Unicorn Knife Fight, and at Bizarro Central.

Stephen Graham Jones started writing in 1990, in an emergency room. Ten years later, his first novel came out, and since then, there have been six more, and two collections. He has also had some hundred and thirty stories published, anthologized, and included in annuals and textbooks. And he still finds himself in the emergency room more than he really planned. Jones teaches in the MFA program at the University of Colorado at Boulder. His novel *Zombie Bake-Off* is forthcoming from Lazy Fascist Press. More at www.demontheory.net.

Len Kuntz is a writer from Washington State. His work appears widely in print and online at such places as Word Riot, PANK, Unicorn Knife Fight, Housefire, elimae, Moon Milk Review, Dogzplot, Decomp, Juked, and MicroHorror. Visit him online at lenkuntz.blogspot.com.

Marc Levinthal was a member of the Grammy-nominated band Green Jello before they were threatened with a lawsuit by Kraft Foods. He is the author of *The Emerald Burrito of Oz* (with John Skipp).

Steve Lowe is a former sports writer with the *South Bend Tribune*, and a sporadic stringer for the Associated Press. These days, instead of sports he writes weird, dark, occasionally humorous fiction which contains slightly more made-up content than his sports stories. His first book, *Muscle Memory*, was published by the Eraserhead Press New Bizarro Author Series. He does not consider the Olive Garden to be real Italian food.

J. David Osborne is the author of the Lynchian gulag-escape novel *By the Time We Leave Here, We'll Be Friends* and *Low Down Death Right Easy*, both published by Swallowdown Press. He lives in Oklahoma with his dog.

Kelli Owen resides in Destination, Pennsylvania with an amazingly talented hippie named Bob Ford and their collection of children and cats. She spends her days paying the bills and her free time writing and/or plotting world domination from the green couch. Her previous titles include the novel *Six Days*, the novella *Waiting Out Winter* (now available as an ebook through Thunderstorm Books), the novella *The Neighborhood* (also available through Thunderstorm), as well as a plethora of shorts, anthologies, and nonfiction pieces. Among the upcoming offerings are two anthologies, two novels, a novella and more. Visit her at www.kelliowen.com for more information.

Poncho Peligroso, 2011 poet laureate of the internet by verdict of Google, is the author of *The Romantic*. His second book, *Ghost Bee Egg*, is forthcoming.

Andersen Prunty is the author of *The Driver's Guide to Hitting Pedestrians*, *My Fake War*, *Zerostrata*, *Morning is Dead*, *Slag Attack*, *Fuckness*, and other books. In 2012 he will conquer the world, or at least steal a globe from some Ohio thrift store. Watch him put his shoes on at www.andersenprunty.com.

Bradley Sands is the author of *Rico Slade Will Fucking Kill You*, *Please Do Not Shoot Me in the Face*, *Sorry I Ruined Your Orgy*, and other books of awkward tragic comedy. He is also the editor of *Bust Down the Door and Eat All the Chickens.*

John Skipp still remains one of America's most cheerfully-perplexing Renaissance mutants: New York Times bestselling author/editor-turned-filmmaker, satirist, cultural crusader, musical pornographer, literary zombie godfather, splatterpunk poster child, Bizarro senior strategist, purveyor of cuddly metaphysics, interpretive dancer, and all-around bon vivant.

Amongst his shitload of books are *The Emerald Burrito of Oz* (with Marc Levinthal); *Spore, The Day Before,* and *Jake's Wake* (with Cody Goodfellow); *The Light at the End, The Bridge,* and *The Scream* (with Craig Spector); and *Stupography, Conscience,* and *The Long Last Call* (by himself). Plus his anthologies *Demons, Zombies, Werewolves and Shapeshifters,* and (with Spector) *Book of the Dead.* He runs Fungasm Press, is editor-in-chief of Ravenous Shadows, and is writer/director/producer of *Rose: The Bizarro Zombie Musical.* He lives in L.A., where he maintains an active lifestyle. He is easily accessible on Facebook.

He also thinks God is most likely delicious.

Bruce Taylor lives in Seattle, Washington. He is the author of *Metamorphosis Blues, Mr. Magic Realism, Kafka's Uncle, Stormworld* (with Brian Herbert), and other books. With Elton Elliott, he co-edited *Like Water for Quarks,* an anthology that explores the intersection of science fiction and magic realism, and features such luminaries as Ursula K. LeGuin, Ray Bradbury, Connie Willis, Greg Bear, and Brian Herbert.

Jeffrey Thomas is the author of *Punktown, Blue War, Letters from Hades, A Nightmare On Elm Street #5: The Dream Dealers,* and *Ugly Heaven, Beautiful Hell* (with Carlton Mellick III).

ABOUT THE COVER ARTIST

Hauke Vagt was born in Hamburg, Germany. In 1997, he relocated to Lisbon, Portugal, where he works as a street painter and freelance illustrator. He has done cover art for other Eraserhead Press books, including *Abortion Arcade* by Cameron Pierce, *Island of the Super People* by Kevin Shamel, and *A Town Called Suckhole* by David W. Barbee.

ABOUT THE ILLUSTRATOR

Dave Brockie, also known as Oderus Urungus, is the lead vocalist of the band GWAR. As Oderus, he has semi-regularly appeared on the Fox News talk show "Red Eye" as the Intergalactic Correspondent. His first novel, *Whargoul*, was published by Deadite Press in 2010. He lives in Pennsylvania.

Bizarro books

CATALOG   SPRING 2011

Bizarro Books publishes under the following imprints:

www.rawdogscreamingpress.com

www.eraserheadpress.com

www.afterbirthbooks.com

www.swallowdownpress.com

For all your Bizarro needs visit:

WWW.BIZARROCENTRAL.COM

Introduce yourselves to the bizarro fiction genre and all of its authors with the Bizarro Starter Kit series. Each volume features short novels and short stories by ten of the leading bizarro authors, designed to give you a perfect sampling of the genre for only $10.

BB-0X1
"The Bizarro Starter Kit"
(Orange)
Featuring D. Harlan Wilson, Carlton Mellick III, Jeremy Robert Johnson, Kevin L Donihe, Gina Ranalli, Andre Duza, Vincent W. Sakowski, Steve Beard, John Edward Lawson, and Bruce Taylor.
236 pages $10

BB-0X2
"The Bizarro Starter Kit"
(Blue)
Featuring Ray Fracalossy, Jeremy C. Shipp, Jordan Krall, Mykle Hansen, Andersen Prunty, Eckhard Gerdes, Bradley Sands, Steve Aylett, Christian TeBordo, and Tony Rauch. **244 pages $10**

BB-0X2
"The Bizarro Starter Kit"
(Purple)
Featuring Russell Edson, Athena Villaverde, David Agranoff, Matthew Revert, Andrew Goldfarb, Jeff Burk, Garrett Cook, Kris Saknussemm, Cody Goodfellow, and Cameron Pierce **264 pages $10**

BB-001 **"The Kafka Effekt" D. Harlan Wilson** - A collection of forty-four irreal short stories loosely written in the vein of Franz Kafka, with more than a pinch of William S. Burroughs sprinkled on top. **211 pages $14**

BB-002 **"Satan Burger" Carlton Mellick III** - The cult novel that put Carlton Mellick III on the map ... Six punks get jobs at a fast food restaurant owned by the devil in a city violently overpopulated by surreal alien cultures. **236 pages $14**

BB-003 **"Some Things Are Better Left Unplugged" Vincent Sakwoski** - Join The Man and his Nemesis, the obese tabby, for a nightmare roller coaster ride into this postmodern fantasy. **152 pages $10**

BB-004 **"Shall We Gather At the Garden?" Kevin L Donihe** - Donihe's Debut novel. Midgets take over the world, The Church of Lionel Richie vs. The Church of the Byrds, plant porn and more! **244 pages $14**

BB-005 **"Razor Wire Pubic Hair" Carlton Mellick III** - A genderless humandildo is purchased by a razor dominatrix and brought into her nightmarish world of bizarre sex and mutilation. **176 pages $11**

BB-006 **"Stranger on the Loose" D. Harlan Wilson** - The fiction of Wilson's 2nd collection is planted in the soil of normalcy, but what grows out of that soil is a dark, witty, otherworldly jungle... **228 pages $14**

BB-007 **"The Baby Jesus Butt Plug" Carlton Mellick III** - Using clones of the Baby Jesus for anal sex will be the hip sex fetish of the future. **92 pages $10**

BB-008 **"Fishyfleshed" Carlton Mellick III** - The world of the past is an illogical flatland lacking in dimension and color, a sick-scape of crispy squid people wandering the desert for no apparent reason. **260 pages $14**

BB-009 "Dead Bitch Army" Andre Duza - Step into a world filled with racist teenagers, cannibals, 100 warped Uncle Sams, automobiles with razor-sharp teeth, living graffiti, and a pissed-off zombie bitch out for revenge. **344 pages $16**

BB-010 "The Menstruating Mall" Carlton Mellick III - "The Breakfast Club meets Chopping Mall as directed by David Lynch." - Brian Keene **212 pages $12**

BB-011 "Angel Dust Apocalypse" Jeremy Robert Johnson - Meth-heads, man-made monsters, and murderous Neo-Nazis. "Seriously amazing short stories..." - Chuck Palahniuk, author of Fight Club **184 pages $11**

BB-012 "Ocean of Lard" Kevin L Donihe / Carlton Mellick III - A parody of those old Choose Your Own Adventure kid's books about some very odd pirates sailing on a sea made of animal fat. **176 pages $12**

BB-015 "Foop!" Chris Genoa - Strange happenings are going on at Dactyl, Inc, the world's first and only time travel tourism company.
"A surreal pie in the face!" - Christopher Moore **300 pages $14**

BB-020 "Punk Land" Carlton Mellick III - In the punk version of Heaven, the anarchist utopia is threatened by corporate fascism and only Goblin, Mortician's sperm, and a blue-mohawked female assassin named Shark Girl can stop them. **284 pages $15**

BB-021 "Pseudo-City" D. Harlan Wilson - Pseudo-City exposes what waits in the bathroom stall, under the manhole cover and in the corporate boardroom, all in a way that can only be described as mind-bogglingly irreal. **220 pages $16**

BB-023 "Sex and Death In Television Town" Carlton Mellick III - In the old west, a gang of hermaphrodite gunslingers take refuge from a demon plague in Telos: a town where its citizens have televisions instead of heads. **184 pages $12**

BB-027 "Siren Promised" Jeremy Robert Johnson & Alan M Clark
- Nominated for the Bram Stoker Award. A potent mix of bad drugs, bad dreams, brutal bad guys, and surreal/incredible art by Alan M. Clark. **190 pages $13**

BB-030 "Grape City" Kevin L. Donihe - More Donihe-style comedic bizarro about a demon named Charles who is forced to work a minimum wage job on Earth after Hell goes out of business. **108 pages $10**

BB-031"Sea of the Patchwork Cats" Carlton Mellick III - A quiet dreamlike tale set in the ashes of the human race. For Mellick enthusiasts who also adore The Twilight Zone. **112 pages $10**

BB-032 "Extinction Journals" Jeremy Robert Johnson - An uncanny voyage across a newly nuclear America where one man must confront the problems associated with loneliness, insane dieties, radiation, love, and an ever-evolving cockroach suit with a mind of its own. **104 pages $10**

BB-034 "The Greatest Fucking Moment in Sports" Kevin L. Donihe
- In the tradition of the surreal anti-sitcom Get A Life comes a tale of triumph and agape love from the master of comedic bizarro. **108 pages $10**

BB-035 "The Troublesome Amputee" John Edward Lawson - Disturbing verse from a man who truly believes nothing is sacred and intends to prove it. **104 pages $9**

BB-037 "The Haunted Vagina" Carlton Mellick III - It's difficult to love a woman whose vagina is a gateway to the world of the dead. **132 pages $10**

BB-042 "Teeth and Tongue Landscape" Carlton Mellick III - On a planet made out of meat, a socially-obsessive monophobic man tries to find his place amongst the strange creatures and communities that he comes across. **110 pages $10**

BB-043 **"War Slut" Carlton Mellick III** - Part "1984," part "Waiting for Godot," and part action horror video game adaptation of John Carpenter's "The Thing." **116 pages $10**

BB-045 **"Dr. Identity" D. Harlan Wilson** - Follow the Dystopian Duo on a killing spree of epic proportions through the irreal postcapitalist city of Bliptown where time ticks sideways, artificial Bug-Eyed Monsters punish citizens for consumer-capitalist lethargy, and ultraviolence is as essential as a daily multivitamin. **208 pages $15**

BB-047 **"Sausagey Santa" Carlton Mellick III** - A bizarro Christmas tale featuring Santa as a piratey mutant with a body made of sausages. 124 pages $10

BB-048 **"Misadventures in a Thumbnail Universe" Vincent Sakowski** - Dive deep into the surreal and satirical realms of neo-classical Blender Fiction, filled with television shoes and flesh-filled skies. **120 pages $10**

BB-049 **"Vacation" Jeremy C. Shipp** - Blueblood Bernard Johnson leaved his boring life behind to go on The Vacation, a year-long corporate sponsored odyssey. But instead of seeing the world, Bernard is captured by terrorists, becomes a key figure in secret drug wars, and, worse, doesn't once miss his secure American Dream. **160 pages $14**

BB-053 **"Ballad of a Slow Poisoner" Andrew Goldfarb** Millford Mutter-wurst sat down on a Tuesday to take his afternoon tea, and made the unpleasant discovery that his elbows were becoming flatter. **128 pages $10**

BB-055 **"Help! A Bear is Eating Me" Mykle Hansen** - The bizarro, heart-warming, magical tale of poor planning, hubris and severe blood loss... **150 pages $11**

BB-056 **"Piecemeal June" Jordan Krall** - A man falls in love with a living sex doll, but with love comes danger when her creator comes after her with crab-squid assassins. **90 pages $9**

BB-058 **"The Overwhelming Urge" Andersen Prunty** - A collection of bizarro tales by Andersen Prunty. **150 pages $11**

BB-059 **"Adolf in Wonderland" Carlton Mellick III** - A dreamlike adventure that takes a young descendant of Adolf Hitler's design and sends him down the rabbit hole into a world of imperfection and disorder. **180 pages $11**

BB-061 **"Ultra Fuckers" Carlton Mellick III** - Absurdist suburban horror about a couple who enter an upper middle class gated community but can't find their way out. **108 pages $9**

BB-062 **"House of Houses" Kevin L. Donihe** - An odd man wants to marry his house. Unfortunately, all of the houses in the world collapse at the same time in the Great House Holocaust. Now he must travel to House Heaven to find his departed fiancee. **172 pages $11**

BB-064 **"Squid Pulp Blues" Jordan Krall** - In these three bizarro-noir novellas, the reader is thrown into a world of murderers, drugs made from squid parts, deformed gun-toting veterans, and a mischievous apocalyptic donkey. **204 pages $12**

BB-065 **"Jack and Mr. Grin" Andersen Prunty** - "When Mr. Grin calls you can hear a smile in his voice. Not a warm and friendly smile, but the kind that seizes your spine in fear. You don't need to pay your phone bill to hear it. That smile is in every line of Prunty's prose." - Tom Bradley. **208 pages $12**

BB-066 **"Cybernetrix" Carlton Mellick III** - What would you do if your normal everyday world was slowly mutating into the video game world from Tron? **212 pages $12**

BB-072 **"Zerostrata" Andersen Prunty** - Hansel Nothing lives in a tree house, suffers from memory loss, has a very eccentric family, and falls in love with a woman who runs naked through the woods every night. **144 pages $11**

BB-073 "The Egg Man" Carlton Mellick III - It is a world where humans reproduce like insects. Children are the property of corporations, and having an enormous ten-foot brain implanted into your skull is a grotesque sexual fetish. Mellick's industrial urban dystopia is one of his darkest and grittiest to date. **184 pages $11**

BB-074 "Shark Hunting in Paradise Garden" Cameron Pierce - A group of strange humanoid religious fanatics travel back in time to the Garden of Eden to discover it is infested with hundreds of giant flying man-eating sharks. **150 pages $10**

BB-075 "Apeshit" Carlton Mellick III - Friday the 13th meets Visitor Q. Six hipster teens go to a cabin in the woods inhabited by a deformed killer. An incredibly fucked-up parody of B-horror movies with a bizarro slant. **192 pages $12**

BB-076 "Fuckers of Everything on the Crazy Shitting Planet of the Vomit At smosphere" Mykle Hansen - Three bizarro satires. Monster Cocks, Journey to the Center of Agnes Cuddlebottom, and Crazy Shitting Planet. **228 pages $12**

BB-077 "The Kissing Bug" Daniel Scott Buck - In the tradition of Roald Dahl, Tim Burton, and Edward Gorey, comes this bizarro anti-war children's story about a bohemian conenose kissing bug who falls in love with a human woman. **116 pages $10**

BB-078 "MachoPoni" Lotus Rose - It's My Little Pony... *Bizarro* style! A long time ago Poniworld was split in two. On one side of the Jagged Line is the Pastel Kingdom, a magical land of music, parties, and positivity. On the other side of the Jagged Line is Dark Kingdom inhabited by an army of undead ponies. **148 pages $11**

BB-079 "The Faggiest Vampire" Carlton Mellick III - A Roald Dahl-esque children's story about two faggy vampires who partake in a mustache competition to find out which one is truly the faggiest. **104 pages $10**

BB-080 "Sky Tongues" Gina Ranalli - The autobiography of Sky Tongues, the biracial hermaphrodite actress with tongues for fingers. Follow her strange life story as she rises from freak to fame. **204 pages $12**

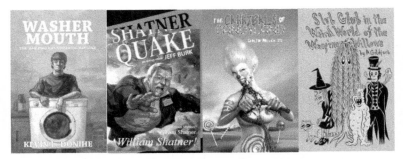

BB-081 **"Washer Mouth" Kevin L. Donihe** - A washing machine becomes human and pursues his dream of meeting his favorite soap opera star. **244 pages $11**

BB-082 **"Shatnerquake" Jeff Burk** - All of the characters ever played by William Shatner are suddenly sucked into our world. Their mission: hunt down and destroy the real William Shatner. **100 pages $10**

BB-083 **"The Cannibals of Candyland" Carlton Mellick III** - There exists a race of cannibals that are made of candy. They live in an underground world made out of candy. One man has dedicated his life to killing them all. **170 pages $11**

BB-084 **"Slub Glub in the Weird World of the Weeping Willows" Andrew Goldfarb** - The charming tale of a blue glob named Slub Glub who helps the weeping willows whose tears are flooding the earth. There are also hyenas, ghosts, and a voodoo priest **100 pages $10**

BB-085 **"Super Fetus" Adam Pepper** - Try to abort this fetus and he'll kick your ass! **104 pages $10**

BB-086 **"Fistful of Feet" Jordan Krall** - A bizarro tribute to spaghetti westerns, featuring Cthulhu-worshipping Indians, a woman with four feet, a crazed gunman who is obsessed with sucking on candy, Syphilis-ridden mutants, sexually transmitted tattoos, and a house devoted to the freakiest fetishes. **228 pages $12**

BB-087 **"Ass Goblins of Auschwitz" Cameron Pierce** - It's Monty Python meets Nazi exploitation in a surreal nightmare as can only be imagined by Bizarro author Cameron Pierce. **104 pages $10**

BB-088 **"Silent Weapons for Quiet Wars" Cody Goodfellow** - "This is high-end psychological surrealist horror meets bottom-feeding low-life crime in a techno-thrilling science fiction world full of Lovecraft and magic..." -John Skipp **212 pages $12**

BB-089 **"Warrior Wolf Women of the Wasteland" Carlton Mellick III**
Road Warrior Werewolves versus McDonaldland Mutants...post-apocalyptic fiction has
never been quite like this. **316 pages $13**

BB-090 **"Cursed" Jeremy C Shipp** - The story of a group of characters who
believe they are cursed and attempt to figure out who cursed them and why. A tale of
stylish absurdism and suspenseful horror. **218 pages $15**

BB-091 **"Super Giant Monster Time" Jeff Burk** - A tribute to choose your
own adventures and Godzilla movies. Will you escape the giant monsters that are rampaging
the fuck out of your city and shit? Or will you join the mob of alien-controlled punk rockers
causing chaos in the streets? What happens next depends on you. **188 pages $12**

BB-092 **"Perfect Union" Cody Goodfellow** - "Cronenberg's THE FLY on a
grand scale: human/insect gene-spliced body horror, where the human hive politics are as
shocking as the gore." -John Skipp. **272 pages $13**

BB-093 **"Sunset with a Beard" Carlton Mellick III** - 14 stories of surreal
science fiction. **200 pages $12**

BB-094 **"My Fake War" Andersen Prunty** - The absurd tale of an unlikely soldier
forced to fight a war that, quite possibly, does not exist. It's Rambo meets Waiting for Godot in
this subversive satire of American values and the scope of the human imagination. **128 pages $11**

BB-095 **"Lost in Cat Brain Land" Cameron Pierce** - Sad stories from a surreal world. A fascist mustache, the ghost of Franz Kafka, a desert inside a dead cat. Primordial entities mourn the death of their child. The desperate serve tea to mysterious creatures.
A hopeless romantic falls in love with a pterodactyl. And much more. **152 pages $11**

BB-096 **"The Kobold Wizard's Dildo of Enlightenment +2" Carlton
Mellick III** - A Dungeons and Dragons parody about a group of people who learn they
are only made up characters in an AD&D campaign and must find a way to resist their
nerdy teenaged players and retarded dungeon master in order to survive. 232 **pages $12**

BB-097 **"My Heart Said No, but the Camera Crew Said Yes!" Bradley Sands -** A collection of short stories that are crammed with the delightfully odd and the scurrilously silly. **140 pages $13**

BB-098 **"A Hundred Horrible Sorrows of Ogner Stump" Andrew Goldfarb** - Goldfarb's acclaimed comic series. A magical and weird journey into the horrors of everyday life. **164 pages $11**

BB-099 **"Pickled Apocalypse of Pancake Island" Cameron Pierce** A demented fairy tale about a pickle, a pancake, and the apocalypse. **102 pages $8**

BB-100 **"Slag Attack" Andersen Prunty -** Slag Attack features four visceral, noir stories about the living, crawling apocalypse.A slag is what survivors are calling the slug-like maggots raining from the sky, burrowing inside people, and hollowing out their flesh and their sanity. **148 pages $11**

BB-101 **"Slaughterhouse High" Robert Devereaux -** A place where schools are built with secret passageways, rebellious teens get zippers installed in their mouths and genitals, and once a year, on that special night, one couple is slaughtered and the bits of their bodies are kept as souvenirs. **304 pages $13**

BB-102 **"The Emerald Burrito of Oz" John Skipp & Marc Levinthal** OZ IS REAL! Magic is real! The gate is really in Kansas! And America is finally allowing Earth tourists to visit this weird-ass, mysterious land. But when Gene of Los Angeles heads off for summer vacation in the Emerald City, little does he know that a war is brewing...a war that could destroy both worlds. **280 pages $13**

BB-103 **"The Vegan Revolution... with Zombies" David Agranoff** When there's no more meat in hell, the vegans will walk the earth. **160 pages $11**

BB-104 **"The Flappy Parts" Kevin L Donihe -** Poems about bunnies, LSD, and police abuse. You know, things that matter. 132 **pages $11**

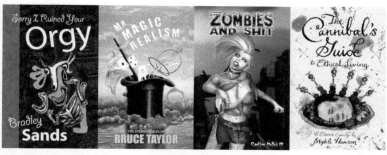

BB-105 **"Sorry I Ruined Your Orgy" Bradley Sands** - Bizarro humorist Bradley Sands returns with one of the strangest, most hilarious collections of the year. **130 pages $11**

BB-106 **"Mr. Magic Realism" Bruce Taylor** - Like Golden Age science fiction comics written by Freud, *Mr. Magic Realism* is a strange, insightful adventure that spans the furthest reaches of the galaxy, exploring the hidden caverns in the hearts and minds of men, women, aliens, and biomechanical cats. **152 pages $11**

BB-107 **"Zombies and Shit" Carlton Mellick III** - "Battle Royale" meets "Return of the Living Dead." Mellick's bizarro tribute to the zombie genre. **308 pages $13**

BB-108 **"The Cannibal's Guide to Ethical Living" Mykle Hansen** - Over a five star French meal of fine wine, organic vegetables and human flesh, a lunatic delivers a witty, chilling, disturbingly sane argument in favor of eating the rich.. **184 pages $11**

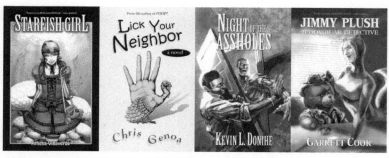

BB-109 **"Starfish Girl" Athena Villaverde** - In a post-apocalyptic underwater dome society, a girl with a starfish growing from her head and an assassin with sea anemone hair are on the run from a gang of mutant fish men. **160 pages $11**

BB-110 **"Lick Your Neighbor" Chris Genoa** - Mutant ninjas, a talking whale, kung fu masters, maniacal pilgrims, and an alcoholic clown populate Chris Genoa's surreal, darkly comical and unnerving reimagining of the first Thanksgiving. **303 pages $13**

BB-111 **"Night of the Assholes" Kevin L. Donihe** - A plague of assholes is infecting the countryside. Normal everyday people are transforming into jerks, snobs, dicks, and douchebags. And they all have only one purpose: to make your life a living hell.. **192 pages $11**

BB-112 **"Jimmy Plush, Teddy Bear Detective" Garrett Cook** - Hardboiled cases of a private detective trapped within a teddy bear body. **180 pages $11**

CPSIA information can be obtained
at www.ICGtesting.com
Printed in the USA
BVHW08s0346160618
519073BV00002BA/100/P